Sacred Drama

Sacred Drama

A Spirituality of Christian Liturgy

Patricia Wilson-Kastner

Fortress Press

Minneapolis

SACRED DRAMA
A Spirituality of Christian Liturgy

Cover design: Graphiculture/Cheryl Watson
Cover art: Nick Markell, Markell Studios, Minneapolis
Interior design: Beth Wright

Library of Congress Cataloging-in-Publication Data

Wilson-Kastner, Patricia.
    Sacred drama : a spirituality of Christian liturgy / Patricia
Wilson-Kastner.
         p.   cm.
    Includes bibliographical references.
    ISBN 0-8006-2604-4
    1. Liturgics.   I. Title.
BV176.W54   1999
264—dc21   99-20324
                                                             CIP

The paper used in this publication meets the minimum requirements for American National Standard for Information Sciences—Permanence of Paper for Printed Library Materials, ANSI Z329.48–1984.

Manufactured in the U.S.A.   AF 1-2604
  03   02   01   00   99   1   2   3   4   5   6   7   8   9   10

Contents

Prologue
Praying the Liturgy, Each Day and Forever

Virginia Everypriest arrived hopefully on the steps of her new church, St. Mary Magdalene-by-the-Tarpits. The interviews had been cheerful but restrained, as though many important thoughts were being saved until another, safer time. All that was needed in the parish was a bit more outreach and lots of evangelism, the search committee had agreed. The parish had entered into a slow but steady numerical decline a few years ago, and everyone assured the rector-to-be that all the parish needed was a bit of firm, involved leadership, and everything would be once again flourishing at St. Magdalene's.

Everyone on the search committee that chose Everypriest as the rector of St. Magdalene's had visited St. Peter's, her former parish. They praised the liturgy there and were delighted with the community involvement in worship and outreach. "Just create that spirit here," said one of the committee members. Virginia Everypriest knew that nothing is ever that simple, but assumed that everything would proceed apace as parishioners and priest prayed and worked together in faith and charity.

There was the rub: prayer. Liturgical prayer, specifically. In accordance with the policy of the diocese, the new priest had read bulletins and talked to parishioners but had never actually participated in a liturgy at St. Magdalene's. A candidate's presence at the liturgy was understood to create undue influence on the parish. So Everypriest would be involved in the parish's liturgy for the first time tomorrow at eleven o'clock, for the Sung Eucharist. She had been assured that the parish was "high church" and asked if she could sing the liturgy. Of course, she replied, going by the old liturgical principle that we do our honest best, and God and the community's spirit of prayer (and its charity) supply for any individual's inadequacies.

The liturgy on Sunday was a shock for the new rector—not simply because everything was sung, even the announcements, it seemed. In the sacristy and the vestibule, all the talk seemed to be about a perfect performance. The subdeacon assured the rector, "God wants perfection in the liturgy. The more solemn it is, the better God likes it." The assistant behaved like a wind-up doll. When the infant twins in the back row (thank heaven some people put up with the mess and complication of having children!) began to cry during the Agnus Dei, Father Pious, the Perpetual Assistant, gazed solemnly up to heaven and then glared at the timorous mother. She grabbed bottles and diapers and was never seen again.

The altar and sanctuary were crowded with clergy and lay people, all vested to the teeth. (The rector later learned that at least half of them wanted to be priests. They also termed themselves "God's special people," as distinct from the rest of the congregation.) The people in the pews were allowed to sing hymns (which the rector was later informed by the music director were "not really part of the service") and some of the simple responses. All else was done by the vested people. The choir was, of course, vested in clerical-looking albs.

No collection was taken up, because, as the rector was later told, money was dirty, and the good people in the parish felt sick if it were on the altar with the Blessed Sacrament. (The rector wasn't feeling too well at this point, either.) What did the children do in the liturgy? Nothing, she was assured, because they might not do it right, and that would distract people. The trained adults did everything. "Oh," replied the rector, baffled.

No wonder, as the parish's real inner life unfolded before the rector, that a major part of the leadership really didn't want to do outreach. They firmly believed that the world was bad and sinful. Church was the place you went to hide from the world, and the better you were the more time you spent in church, safe from the world's evil. Why reach out to the world?

What did the strange new rector expect them to do? Preach and pray as if the liturgy were being prayed in the world, to nourish and strengthen people for mission? Sing fewer things in the liturgy to make it simpler for people? Get the children involved? Make the offering of alms and oblations a part of the liturgy, putting money on God's altar? Have fewer vested people, and perhaps act as if lay people at the liturgy were as important as clergy? Horrors! God liked worship solemn, sung, and as removed from the world as possible. The world and God's worship were two distinct and separate realities.

When she recovered from her surprise, Virginia Everypriest mustered up some sympathy. After all, she had attended those liturgies that seemed not like the worship of God, but the celebration of the congregation's self. She not-so-fondly recalled one momentous Easter Day Eucharist several years earlier. Because the Vigil was the major service at her church, St. Peter's, she went incognito to attend St. Jude's-by-the-Gas-Pump, where she had been invited to preach on the Third Sunday of Easter. The liturgy (or so it was called) began with a crash of guitars, an incomprehensible hymn projected on the wall behind the altar, and an ambling procession in which everyone, including all the clergy, was wearing bunny ears. (I regret to say that I am *not* making this up!)

The sermon centered on the Resurrection as the great feast of the hope we humans had within us. Just as the grass grew green again after the blasts of winter, we could recover from the tragedies and sufferings that were a natural part of the human condition. Children from bad neighborhoods could go to college and become happy, productive citizens; people who experienced serious illnesses could laugh and find health again; and those who mourned the death of loved ones could find others to love and with whom to rejoice. Virginia Everypriest sat attentively, waiting to hear what this Jesus fellow had to do with such naive cheerful interpretations of the world, or how tombs and crosses were connected with Easter morning, but those were never referred to. Suddenly the sermon ended in a burst of joy about the new generation who were the resurrection of our hopes and expectations, and then the congregation rushed into the Prayers of the People.

Someone began them with an invocation to the "God of Affirmative Action and Positive Vibes." Everypriest was certain she was having a flashback to the '60s, but as she bit her tongue, she realized that it was the 1990s, and she still stood in the pew at St. Jude's, her hands grasped by her neighbors on both sides. (Goodness, how had that happened?) As the organ sounded for the offertory, all the children lined up at the back in their new clothes. After the collection had been taken, the children came up to the altar, bearing painted eggs, which they handed to acolytes, who placed them in a basket before the cross. Then, literally with a roll of the trumpets, the priest elevated the alms basin, while everyone joined vigorously in the doxology. In the background, a timid acolyte hesitantly offered the bread and wine to the assisting priest.

At that point Virginia Everypriest felt overwhelmed and quickly exited the church. As she recovered outside in the quiet, cool air, she asked the friendly greeter about when the liturgy brought up such little matters as God, creation in God's image, the body of Christ, responsibility for one another, sin, forgiveness, suffering, death, eternal life. Did the members of the parish try to evangelize and bring into their parish the quite impoverished and struggling people from the housing project just up the street? He looked at Everypriest as though she were speaking in a foreign tongue, and offered her a set of bunny ears as an Easter remembrance of the parish.

As you have probably guessed, neither Virginia Everypriest nor I was happy about either of these liturgies. Even less were we pleased about the ways in which those liturgies both reflected and idealized very unbiblical, indeed unchristian ways of living out Christian commitment in everyday life. The problem in both situations, which I have obviously painted in broad and overdramatized brushstrokes, is that liturgy falsely represented the relationship between God and the community. In the first case, a world-denying "high church" liturgy failed to help people relate their own individual lives to God, much less to the hopes and dreams of the world in which they lived. In the second case, the liturgy refused to take seriously either God and the transcendent dimension of all life, or the complexity of the human community and our need for redemption, healing, and reconciliation, as well as affirmation.

Each approach to liturgy was radically unchristian in its roots and totally inadequate to the fullness of Christian corporate worship. What is the essence of liturgy? What is the true "heart of the matter" in worship, that nourishes Christians with the Word of God, in Scripture proclaimed and bread and wine shared? How does worship rightly and freely entered into both feed and empower us to live as Christians in the world? How do Word and Sacrament animate each other as one transforming gracious event?

A few simple assumptions underlie this book. The first is that the altar and the world are profoundly interconnected; indeed, in God's eye they are two dimensions of the one reality of our human life as creatures of God. The second assumption is that the sermon is an integral part of the liturgy, and that it has the same basic shape or plot as the whole liturgy: gathering the people of God together, letting the common reality of our lives encounter the transforming grace of God in the Scriptures, and going forth into the world to share the transforming grace received. A third supposition is that the liturgy, particularly articulated in the homily or sermon, is the locus for the identity-formation of the Christian community. That is, in worship we receive our sense of who we are as Christians, and we struggle to express our faith and grow in our relationships as members of Christ's body living in the world.

Grounded in these assumptions, this book explores Sunday eucharistic liturgy as the distinctive and central way in which we are shaped and nurtured in our identity as Christians and grow in that identity as the transformed and transforming people of God. I have written it to articulate my belief that the liturgy, if it is true to itself, both reflects and embodies the world as God made us to be. The way we pray the liturgy expresses our faith and hope in God's new creation, and the love by which we both grow and are recreated into God's people.

I.
The Liturgy as Sacred Drama
Its Shape and Movement

The Shape of the Liturgy

Over fifty years ago, Gregory Dix wrote a weighty but lively tome titled *The Shape of the Liturgy.* In his introduction, Dix asserted that he wrote to illuminate the most central and important "ritual pattern" of the Christian community—the Eucharist. He contends that we Christians have formed essentially one ritual with a unified dynamic movement, capable of varied adaptations to different peoples and cultures.

The liturgical venture undertaken by Dix was not intended simply to dazzle his readers with his scholarly grasp of two thousand years' worth of liturgy. His work addresses our contemporary problem of the "individual's relationship to society and his need for and securing of material things." Dix insists that the Eucharist offers the "Christian pattern of a solution." In the Eucharist, he argues, the individual is perfectly integrated into society and finds his or her needs for material goods met, not denied. In the Eucharist our needs are met, not by what we can take from each other, but by the resources of our world "freely offered by each of its members for all."[1]

Dix assumed that there is an essentially unified structure of the Eucharist that has been, and is being, embellished in many ways in many different cultures. This shape or movement of the liturgy is God's gift to us, not just to transform us as individuals, but to recreate us as children of God and dwellers in God's realm, which is "on earth as it is in heaven."

Thus liturgy is a response to the chaos and contingency of life as we experience it. Granted this purpose of liturgy, let us shift the focus slightly from Dix's formulation. In individual conversations and over international media, we humans directly and covertly question whether life has any meaning at all, whether we have any responsibility for each other, and whether there is any hope for our future. In the liturgy, the Christian community poses these questions and offers a response to the world. Liturgy offers shape and purpose for the life of the world. In the liturgy, both individual life and community existence are integrated in a common expression of faith. Liturgy is the core expression of our personal and corporate identity.[2]

Liturgy: What Is It?

Both a world-denying appraoch and an uncritically world-affirming approach to worship fail to grasp and to express the heart of liturgy, its being, meaning, and purpose for us. It is to that heart that I wish to direct our attention, because it will give us our vision of the church as liturgical community, and what our liturgy is and can be. Within the context of liturgy, we can clarify and strengthen our understanding of preaching—how it is related to the liturgy and the ways in which it moves in harmony with the entire liturgy to proclaim God's Word to each specific worshiping community.

What is liturgy? The English word comes from "the work of the people" in Greek. What kind of work? Who are the people? Originally in Greek the phrase did not mean "a work done by lots of people," but some work undertaken for the community's good (a public philanthropy). Building a bridge, doing military service, or putting on a public play was "liturgy." The Septuagint translators used "liturgy" to describe the Temple worship. In the New Testament, "liturgy" identified Temple worship, but also received a uniquely Christian meaning—Jesus' life and obedient death for us, and his risen life for our redemption (see Heb. 8:6). Thus the Christian life lived in the spirit of Jesus is also a liturgy (see Phil. 2:30).[3]

Therefore the theological and spiritual origin of Christian liturgy is the life of Christ and our sharing in his life as members of the body of Christ. That is the root of the Christian meaning of liturgy. But in common discourse we have also retained and today almost always use the word *liturgy* to mean a public service of worship in the Christian community. The Episcopalian, for example, who picks up a copy of *Liturgy for Living* in the Church's Teaching Series will quite reasonably expect the volume to address the contemporary Christian understanding of worship, with its rich tradition of two thousand years of corporate prayer.

For the community that gathers to reflect, pray to God, share with one another, and be changed in and through the Spirit of God, it is important to hold both profoundly interrelated meanings in mind: liturgy is Christ's and our life together, and liturgy is public worship. Geoffrey Wainwright has described worship as "the point of concentration in which the whole of the Christian life comes into ritual focus."[4] All of life—past, present, and to come—is drawn together for the Christian through this ritual action. Christian liturgy is always focused, overtly or less directly, through Jesus Christ and the church of Christ.

The connection between the two verbal meanings of *liturgy* can be made, because in the liturgy the "church is manifesting, creating, and fulfilling herself [*sic*] as the Body of Christ."[5] The liturgy as the church's worship is the action through which it receives its nature from God through Christ's gracious self-giving. In liturgy, the church receives God's gift—boundless love—and expresses it in word and action as a praying community in the world.

In the liturgy, the community expresses its most profound identity, that of God's people. In this community, each member is given an identity as one of God's people and also learns to shape her or his identity within this community in the world. Through liturgy, the church articulates its life and mission, its relation to God and to the world. In that sense it gives identity to its members—an identity that is corporate, never individual. Because each person is unique, with particular gifts, challenges, and contributions to make in particular times and places, the shared identity will always be realized by each person in a different way.

Liturgy as Worship. What is the primary character of this cultic action? Liturgy, from this perspective, is the form the people of God follow when they meet together for public worship. It can range from the pageantry of Solemn Pontifical High Mass at St. Peter's Basilica to the silence of the Friends' Meeting House in Lower East Side in Manhattan. Variety is the hallmark of liturgy as worship, and it is particularly characteristic of Protestant Christianity.[6] Through any number of different actions, songs, readings, prayers, silent and spoken reflections, sharing the bread and wine at the eucharistic table, and other sacramental acts, the community acts out its identity and through God's love is confirmed in that identity, is corrected, strengthened, and transformed in its identity, and thus grows in its internal relationships and its relationships to the world and to God.

From a descriptive perspective, the above comments are absolutely true. However, I firmly believe that Christian liturgy is more than simply self-identified acts of public worship by Christians. Theological evaluation impels us to ask, What is the core of liturgy? Is it whatever Christians do when they pray together, or is it a particular sort of public worship? Liturgy thus envisioned is both what Christians do according to their own cultural and temperamental gifts and aspirations and what the community believes that God through Jesus Christ has asked them to do in worship.

No one would be so naive as to assume that before the ascension Jesus handed around to the disciples copies of the *Book of Common Prayer* or the Liturgy of St. John Chrysostom (or any other form). However, there is a firm tradition, which goes as deeply as can be traced into the church's roots, that Baptism and Eucharist are central and essential to Christian worship. "Go and teach all nations, baptizing them . . ." and "do this in remembrance of me" are almost certainly not literally dominical words, but they reflect the profound and early conviction of the church that initiation through water and Jesus' spirit and the sharing of bread and wine blessed in Jesus' name were the primary cultic acts constituting the Christian community, and were received by the church through the example and spirit of Jesus.

From the earliest days of the church, Sunday Eucharist has been assumed as the constituting and normative act of worship (1 Cor. 11–12; Didache XIV). Eucharist is the norm and nourishment of the community and its worship, "the central act of Christian worship,"[7] and the ordinary worship of Christians on the Lord's Day.[8] No matter how simply or how elaborately celebrated, in what cultural guise, or in what physical setting it takes place, the Christian community from its inception has been rooted in "the breaking of the bread and the prayers" (Acts 2:42). That eucharistic centrality of Christian worship is a historical link with the communion of saints throughout the ages.[9] Today it is increasingly acknowledged in the churches as essential for the community's self-awareness and expression of its own identity.[10]

Liturgy, the work of the people, centers itself in the Eucharist, the work of all God's people, in their character as a community called by God, not simply as isolated individuals. As Dom Gregory Dix so aptly phrases it, "Liturgy is the name given . . . to the act of taking part in the solemn corporate worship of God by the 'priestly' society of Christians

who are 'the Body of Christ, the church.' "[11] Vital and important as personal prayer is, it receives its nourishment and fulfills its role as an
expression of our life in the church as members of the body of Christ.
In this sense, all prayer grows out of our life as God's priestly people
and is centered in worship. All prayer, corporate or private, expresses
the eucharistic worship of the baptized community in all elements of
its life in time and space. In God all prayer, individual or corporate,
free or fixed, is one in its reaching to the divine. For the Christian,
the source and unity of all our prayer is the liturgy of the baptized
community.

From the Christian perspective, liturgical worship, because it is the
worship of a community, necessarily is embodied, sacramental, and
"worldly." What Aidan Kavanagh declared about liturgical theology
is even more true of the liturgy on which the theology is based:

> Since the notion of worship is sacramental throughout . . . the world
> is included at the very core of what founds or establishes the belief
> upon which theology reflects. . . . Take the created world, with all
> its intractable ambiguities, out of a theological statement and the
> result is not the way things are in orthodox Christian faith.[12]

Worship is at its heart "worldly" because it expresses the intussuscep-
tion of the church and the Gospel into the world like yeast into the
bread. In the parable, we note, the church is like the yeast in the bread
(Matt. 13:33). Once the yeast is mixed into the bread, it becomes
inseparable from the bread. We no longer find yeast and bread, only
one reality, yeast-in-bread.

Alexander Schmemann laments those Christians who falsely think
that worship is time to hide from the world, a vent for grace to be
poured into us from heaven. Instead, worship is the church's evidenc-
ing of its character as the leaven in the loaf, the love of God in the
world, the witness to God's reign, new life for the universe.[13] The
liturgy thus is not worship of God by Christians who have withdrawn
into an otherworldly sphere; it is the ritualized expression of the interconnection of God with the world through the church.

Bernard Iddings Bell, in the *Altar and the World,* articulated the
essentially worldly and social dimensions of the liturgy:

> The Liturgy has social implications. More than that, its social
> aspects are its fundamental aspect; it is a corporate worship, the
> worship of a band of brothers [*sic*] sworn to high adventure with

> their Lord, adventure which is social, the loving of the world into
> goodness until the kingdoms of that world are become the king-
> doms of our God and of His Christ.[14]

In somewhat florid late Victorian tones, Bell identified a fundamental element of liturgy: It is social not just because lots of people are involved, but because we all participate through our worship and our life in a corporate enterprise with cosmic dimensions. Individualism or factionalism is utterly contrary to the very nature of liturgy. Furthermore, the act of worship is never in isolation from life because liturgy is the expression of a community's faith as well as an act that empowers Christians to engage in a life embodying God's loving will for the world.

For the Christian community, liturgy is the ritual form of the interconnection of God and the world, as believed and lived in and through that community. We give corporate, dramatic shape to our aspirations for our own individual transformation and that of the whole world. As we struggle to articulate our present identity and our vision of our future, we use gestures and words to grapple with the interconnection of God, humanity, and world; express the complex dimensions of this relationship (dependence, alienation, reconciliation); and articulate the Christian community's role in a history, with its own unique moments in each time and place.

Our aspirations are deeply spiritual, inasmuch as they seek to express the world's reaching toward God and discovery of God in the world. Liturgy is at the same time essentially worldly because it is about the world's creation and re-creation in God. The Eucharist is quintessentially earthly, because it is overtly in a particular time and space, it is dependent on particular people and things for its celebration, and it celebrates the past, present, and future of a world transformed in and through God's love. The Eucharist is not a worship that flees from the world, but one that sacramentally testifies to God's creative transformation of the earth.

Because eucharistic worship communicates in ritual, concrete form, the human involvement in God's creation and recreation of the world, "drama" is a very useful, if partial, description of liturgical worship. Drama, in its most general sense, is an action, in which "actors imitate for spectators a deed . . . by gestures and/or words."[15] Even apparent chaos or absurdity in the theater arises from a conviction that the drama expresses and gives identifiable shape to the disorder or mean-inglessness of life, so that its true character can be exposed and acknowledged by us. With this acknowledgment, we can live in a more reflective and prepared way, whether or not we can change the world. Thus drama is a representation or mimesis of life, offered in a concen-trated and unified form to an audience, in such a way that the audience identifies with the action and characters and moves from its present understanding to a new perception of an important dimension of life.[16]

Drama as a metaphor for liturgy is not well received by many litur-gists today. Gordon Lathrop, for instance, would prefer to consider liturgy as the weaving together of people, things, actions, and words into patterns of meaning.[17]

There are obvious ways in which liturgy is a drama, with players, costumes, and a plot; others are less obvious. But for the purposes of illuminating the interconnection of liturgy with life, I suggest five ele-ments of Christian liturgy as a dramatic action of the community. Liturgy is mimesis or imitation of life, cultic drama, cosmic, comic, and formed as a sacrificial meal in which everyone participates. Certainly other elements are involved in Christian liturgy as drama (for example, seasons, the variety of forms, and so forth), but these five are most basic.

Liturgy Is an Imitation of Life. The classic description of drama is in Aristotle's *Poetics.* Drama is a representation of life, "an imitation of an action that is serious and . . . complete in itself."[18] Drama is an imita-tion of life. By this Aristotle does not mean simply a "slice of life"; he intends us to understand that drama creates a cogent patterning of human thoughts, feelings, and events that are shaped by the author into an artistic whole. This unity compresses for our reflection and our transformation the most fundamental human realities, with their emotions, thoughts, and motivations; the interconnections among people; and the various developments of specific great events or senti-ments, whether it be the horror of an old man's mistaken perception of love and loyalty in *King Lear,* or the hopelessness of a frustrated life trapping itself into death in *'Night, Mother.*

When we have seen a great play, we come out feeling that we have experienced a catharsis (a cleansing) through seeing some aspect of human life presented to us in its greatness and its potential for disas-ter. We also experience a sigh of recognition, acknowledging that the play may have been about someone else, but it is also about us. If a play is good, something in me identifies myself with all the characters. I remain myself, a member of the audience, but I see myself in the characters, their feelings, and their actions. Thus I bring something to the play and also receive something from it—deeper feelings and understandings, a clearer and more compassionate vision of the human condition. What I receive, through my participation, changes my awareness and therefore my whole self.

Drama is mimesis. Such imitation is not simply a repetition of patterns or actions, but a strategy for coping with the disparity we humans feel between our humanity as it is, in its fragility and brokenness, and the good for which we believe we were made.[19] Mimesis in good drama changes and transforms us by exposing the disparities between what we are and what we might become, and by showing how creative change can occur. Dramatic mimesis is not didactic, telling people how to change, but rather an expressive art form that shows the human condition in all its tensions, uncertainties, and potential for good and evil, and evokes response from us.

The liturgy is always formed as mimetic drama. In the Eucharist, we bring the whole human condition before God—our history, our temptations, the good we do, our needs, our hopes, our fears. Each time we participate, the drama is a bit different, the focus is slightly changed—different liturgical seasons, different readings, new people, individual experiences, community changes—and all these elements add new dimensions to the greatest drama of all.

In the Eucharist, we remember God's creation of the world, our alienation, and our restoration in Christ through the Spirit. Even apparent chaos or absurdity is given place in the drama. Liturgy incorporates, expresses, and gives shape to the perceived chaos and meaninglessness of life, so that we can see its true character, acknowledge its reality in our lives, and interact in a more reflective way with powers we do not understand. We want to discover and share in some form of meaning in our world, even when it is not immediately obvious.

Each time the liturgical drama is performed, at least two key dimensions are present: The fundamental great action of human life is reenacted, and unique lives are also expressed in the liturgy. As I will examine more deeply in the next chapter, liturgy is not timeless and static. Each generation, each performance offers a different Hamlet or Electra, with a different vision and ever new revelations. Even more profound, the people of St. Magdalene's or St. Peter's bring them-selves; their gifts, hopes, and failures; their families and neighbors; and all the people of the world to be a part of the Eucharist. Through the prayers, the actions, the sharing at the altar, each unique world at this present moment is drawn into the great drama. Each time, some-thing different and wonderful occurs for that community as it brings itself to Eucharist and lets the Eucharist interpret what the community is and change it in the telling.

St. Magdalene's parish, for instance, may be composed of primarily young and energetic members, with many people eager to act to change the world and to better their own condition. They will cele-brate the liturgy accordingly, bringing their energy and ambitions to the prayers, the proclaiming of the Word, the sharing of Christ's table, and the dismissal back into the world. But in a true liturgical drama, they will also let the great action shape them to see that their action also involves suffering, attention to those who are not able to compete, and waiting on God's Word to show them compassion and patience before they rush back into the world. What they are becoming and what they have learned about God's world will continually change them and their ongoing celebrations of the Eucharist. Liturgy reflects and is drawn from our lives, but it also reshapes and reforms them through our experience of God's action in the great liturgy of Jesus' death and resurrection for us.

Liturgy Is Cultic Drama. Liturgy is cultic drama in the classic sense of *cultus,* a system of rites for the worship of God. In its most basic sense, every religion, including every Christian group, has a cult—a set of expected ways to worship God. The so-called liturgical churches are the most obviously cultic, but anyone who has attended a revival or even a Quaker meeting knows that groups have set and expected ways of worshiping. Woe betide the conductor of worship or the group that does not meet expectations!

"O Jesus, I just want you to know that I . . . ," the preacher always prays when it is time to testify. *Or:* After the third hymn calling us to return from sin, it is time for someone to come and kneel at the altar. The congregation expects it, and almost every time, someone will come up. *Or:* If the preacher reads a prayer, the congregation will be up in arms; the preacher is supposed to preach and pray without notes—sermon about forty minutes and prayers for ten. *Or:* We must always use prayer 1 of Rite 1, and always have two candles, each one and one-half inches from the edge of the altar. *And so forth.*

Behind the apparent trivialities of the ritual rests a fundamental character of cultic worship: The acts, the words, the interweaving of the elements are expected by the participants in the drama. They are expected to be in a recognizable form because the liturgy is integral and essential to forming and nurturing our identity. Because we are human beings of flesh and blood who live together in community, we need familiar rituals and symbols. By sharing and participating in them, we develop a sense of security and begin to form our identity as members of particular communities.[20]

By sharing regularly in the same cultic rituals and symbols, the community continually reinforces in its members the sense of all being participants. Sometimes what appears to be a small aspect of the liturgy as cult is important to a participant because it is that person's role in the drama. To change the cultic form is to challenge the person's part in the play and the outcome of the drama.

In certain situations, such an action may be appropriate. Plays do need to be rewritten and people's roles changed. The drama of the liturgy has an established essential plot, but the roles of its participants must always be changing, because human awareness of our relation to God and the world is never complete. Thus the key to the change and variability of liturgy is the balance between the inclusion of the people in the community's cult and the changing of life of the community in Christ.

To offer an example, in the Maundy Thursday liturgy, as in all of the Holy Week rites, we Episcopalians have changed rather significantly over the last few years or so. The liturgical renewal movement that began among the Roman Catholics has pressed us to look at our own roots and aspirations as a Christian community. In the 1928 Prayer Book, all that was provided for Holy Week was special propers for the Eucharist. Different groups, especially among the Anglo-Catholics, tried to revive older forms and seek ways to a more meaningful Holy Week liturgy, but the approach was based primarily on resuscitation of nineteenth-century Catholic ritual perceptions of a medieval liturgy that never existed.

At first the development for Maundy Thursday seems a bit unusual and raises questions about how well it might serve as a cultic worship for Episcopalians, who frequently have a justified reputation for resistance to liturgical change. In the new Maundy Thursday liturgy, the washing of the feet follows the sermon and comes before the prayers of the people. There was and still continues to be some resistance to the reintroduction of this old ritual, but after initial embarrassment and uneasiness, many parishes have adapted the ritual of foot-washing cheerfully and readily in a liturgy that speaks of service and self-giving.

Some communities have placed the foot-washing in the context of a meal that is part of the liturgical observance of Maundy Thursday. The reading of the liturgy and its tone of self-sacrifice and self-giving make the foot-washing an eloquent symbol to many people. Even those who would themselves not wish to have their feet washed voice sentiments of appreciation, seeing dramatically the connection with the Last Supper of Jesus and a symbolic reenactment of the Christian commitment to service. Sometime even people's reluctance to have their feet washed has opened them up to recognizing their resistance to allowing others to serve them and their fear of the involvement of the body in worship. These awkward and sometimes painful moments have also freed participants in the liturgy for unexpected change and transformation.

The key to the incorporation of these new elements into cults seems to lie in the congruity of the new elements with what people perceive as an aspect of Christian life essential to the Christian commitment in the body of Christ. The new element of the cultic worship is experienced as expanding the community's identity, expressing aspects of the identity that need to be developed, or opening up dimensions that grow from the community's responding to new situations. Once people can see the relationship (or at least allow that such a relation is possible and that others need to express it in the liturgy), the cultic worship can change.

When such changes arise or are made, they are experienced, except perhaps by small numbers of the people, not as threatening their identity as members of the church, but as strengthening them in becoming who God made them to be. In such a change, the new elements will be experienced by the people as being in harmony with the older or more familiar symbols, and thus expressing the mystery of the Gospel in a better way for the whole church community.

Liturgy Is Cosmic Drama. Historians have traced the roots of drama to the human desire to express our encounter with the sacred and particularly to temple worship in ancient Greece.[21] The scope of the Christian sacred drama encompasses the entirety of the sacred: the whole universe of good and evil, and the divine creator of all. Our liturgy expands the context and the participants well beyond the human struggle with ourselves, our feelings, and our desires, to embrace the entire universe. The players in the drama include God, angelic and demonic powers, humanity and its world, and all the rest of creation, focused in the church, who is, if you will, producing the drama. Sometimes this cosmic scope is explicit, other times implicit, but it is always present.

For an example, let us take the Episcopal Eucharistic Rite II, which begins with an invocation of God and God's kingdom, including angels, archangels, the heavens, all humanity in its various conditions and places in the world, and all the created world. Ordinarily there is some reference to evil and sin, sometimes personified, and always to the evil within us. The intention of the liturgy is to include everything within its scope and to express our human interconnection with God and with the rest of the cosmos.

In the Episcopal Church's *Book of Common Prayer,* the most explicit statement of such cosmic scope is in Prayer D, which is similar to Eucharistic Prayer 4 of the Roman Canon, and has its roots in the Liturgy of John Chrysostom. In the Preface, the Celebrant prays:

> It is truly right to glorify you, O Father and to give you thanks. . . . Fountain of life, you made all things and fill them with your blessing; you created them to rejoice in the splendor of your radiance....Countless throngs of angels stand before you. . . . Joining with them, and giving voice to every creature under heaven, we acclaim you, and glorify your Name. . . .[22]

The new United Church of Christ Service of Word and Sacrament I, liturgy B, gives thanks to the Holy One, begetter of Jesus Christ, "by whom you made the world and all things." The liturgy declares its intent to be cosmic in the most fundamental sense of including everything and every one within its perspective. Thus Jesus is not merely addressed as our redeemer, or friend, or even our crucified and risen Lord. Jesus' role as the incarnate Word of God to humanity is put in context of the sharing of this Word of God in the creation of the universe. The words of this liturgy make quite explicit that its prayer is not just about a congregation and God; it is to God about everyone and everything that is.

The liturgy is also cosmic in its vision of history as the story of the interaction of God and the world in time and space. There have been many different emphases in the eucharistic liturgy,[23] but all of them in some way encompass the history of humanity within God's creative, reconciling, and renewing activity in all creation. The medieval church focused on the cross and at times became dominantly individualistic, but the cosmic scope remained, even if not always articulated or realized. Some of the liturgies of the early church (as in the Didache) or in medieval interpretations were more concerned with an eschatological perspective than the contemporary church tends to be. At the same time, even these earlier liturgies remained aware of the continued importance of the present world, and liturgies that are much concerned with the present are incomplete without an eschatological perspective.[24]

The cosmic scope of liturgy also reminds us that we are not the only players in the drama. The liturgy is a drama focused in the human condition; we do not try to reenact a Christian version of the primordial victory of Marduk over chaos, or Demeter's recovery of Persephone. We are created; Jesus has offered himself on the cross; he is risen and the Holy Spirit dwells among us. In our liturgical drama, which takes the basic form of a sacrificial meal, we remember these great events in our history and let ourselves be reconnected with the present reality of the great cosmic creation and reconciliation of our world with God.

Allegorical tendencies in the Christian tradition have tried to convert the players into stand-ins for God, but the basic shape of the Eucharist makes it utterly clear that such an approach is a dreadful misapprehension of the drama.[25] We are human participants, playing human roles, being ourselves as members of a cosmic community in which creation and redemption take place, and in which we are interconnected, through God's gracious love and our prayer, with all the other sharers in this life together.

Consequently, celebrating the Eucharist as though the priest or minister is God or Jesus and the congregation is ordinary sinful humanity is misleading and false. We are the people of God, repre-

senting the whole of God's world at worship, and some among us take
particular roles within God's people in the Eucharist. The different
roles are important in leading and guiding the people at prayer, so
that the whole people may remember God's gracious works. God is
present invisibly and through Christ in the symbols of bread and
wine. The clergy, assistants, musicians, and other eucharistic ministers, important as their roles are, are no more *alter Christus* in the
Eucharist than other Christians. In the cosmic drama, the cosmic players are all present. The humans in the drama are not playing God or
angels but are acting as humans at prayer in God's universe.[26]

The cosmic perspective of the drama of the liturgy thus has breadth
and depth, including everything from beginning to end of time. But
the event that focuses on drama is not fundamentally a historical
pageant, or even a series of dramatic events portrayed for us. The basic
plot of liturgical drama is shaped within the enactment of a meal.
"Consequently, the Eucharist is a sacramental meal which by visible
signs communicates to us God's love in Jesus Christ, the love by
which Jesus loved his own 'to the end.'"[27] All the other metaphors and
figures for the Eucharist derive from its fundamental character as
sacred meal.

Liturgy Is a Sacrificial Meal. When we walk into a church, the character of the drama as a meal is usually quite evident. The altar is a
table, sometimes an overtly utilitarian one and other times ornate and
even obscured. Historically, the Christian Eucharist derives directly
from a Jewish ritual meal, perhaps the Passover meal, or more likely a
ritual thanksgiving meal.[28]

This eucharistic meal is not, as we have noted already, just any sort
of sacred meal, but a sacrificial meal, in which God offers divine life to
us through Jesus, and we offer our own selves to God.[29] The figure of
the marriage feast of the Lamb (Rev. 19, 7, 9) was frequently used in
the church to draw together the notion of meal, wedding of God and
humanity, and the sacrificial self-giving of the meal. The image also
echoed Passover themes. Thus the liturgy is understood as a meal here
and now that directs the participants toward the eschatological fulfillment of this sacrificial meal. Sacrifice and eschatology are not everyday
words, especially about meals, but in the Eucharist they describe the
primary character of the meal, which is not simply a gathering for
friendship or a food we enjoy.

In the physical arrangements of the church and the appearance of the liturgy, the meal rightly determines the setting for the drama of the liturgy. The altar table is the center around which the drama plays. Pulpit, lectern, baptismal font, seating, and arrangements for kneeling: All are arranged to facilitate the congregation's worship at the Lord's table.

At the beginning of the liturgy, the players are gathered around the table, remember stories of the earlier community, reflect on the present significance of those past events, pray for the needs of all the world, and join together in a meal. Sometimes the meal character is a very formal ritual, like the wedding banquet of a large and distinguished family. At other times, both setting and demeanor speak of an intimate group at table. In any situation, the action of the sacrificial meal is the focal reality of the physical space and the shape of the liturgical action. (This is why a Christian's noncommunicating attendance at the Eucharist is as inappropriate as coming to Sunday dinner and refusing to eat.)

The Scriptures are full of images for the Eucharist as meal, both as present symbolic meal and as the sign of the wedding feast of the Lamb at the end of time. These images of Eucharist as a meal also have ramifications for human ethical behavior. How, for instance, can people who share the same eucharistic banquet allow each other to go hungry, either at the table or in everyday life? In the early church, that question was already raised by Paul with the Corinthians (1 Cor. 11:17-21) and in a more general way by James (2:1-17). Modern works about the Eucharist raise social issues even more explicitly.[30] Eucharistic sharing implies—indeed, necessitates—sharing of all other goods as well. The only question possible is not "whether" but "how." Thus the eucharistic liturgy itself raises the moral and ethical questions about change in the community, as well as incorporating directions for the necessary changes in individual and community.

Liturgy Is Comic Drama. How does the play end? As we watch any good drama, that is the question that intrigues us the most, and keeps us attentive to the end. The Christian liturgical drama is not a tragedy, but a comedy that ends in rebirth and hope.[31] We do not come to the Eucharist to wonder what will happen to us, or to guess if our life has any purpose. We come because deep in our bones, amid all the doubts and uncertainties, amid all the chances and changes of this transitory life, we believe that through Baptism we share in the death and resurrection of Jesus. Our question is: how?

How do our specific lives share in the creation and redemption of the world by God through Jesus Christ? Where is the Holy Spirit in our flesh, our streets, our jobs, our play? In the liturgy we bring ourselves, our souls and bodies, our families and friends, and all of our world, to let ourselves be drawn into the cosmic comedy. We want to feel redemption, to be assured of God's action, even if we can't feel it and touch it right now. Our liturgy needs to connect us, visibly and tangibly, with the assurance that "all will be well, because all is in God's hands."

We can be reassured only if we are assured that God is in charge of the universe and God is the judge who can and will transform the creation into what God intends it to be. God's judgment, in this sense, is acclaimed by prophets and the psalmist as the readiness of God to remake the world. Judgment is both comforting and threatening: comforting because we want a just world, which lives according to God's mercy and faithfulness, but threatening because we know that we ourselves participate in the worldliness that needs to be reformed. The liturgy proclaims the judgment of God as hope and mercy for the world, even if that mercy and hope will also require the world's transformation.

We don't have all the details of the script. In that regard we are involved in something more like improvisational theater. But we are certain of the great movement of the action and through the liturgy are drawn into a vision of the wholeness of creation in God, in order to be assured and strengthened to play our part in reconnecting ourselves and the world with God and each other. Liturgy reconnects us with God and with all creation, rekindles in us the vision of the restoration of all in God, and clarifies and nourishes again in us the hope in which we can live now in justice, peace, and love with each other.

The Role of the Sermon

Gregory Dix argued that the service of the Word (synaxis) and the eucharistic liturgy were originally two separate services, joined together primarily for practical reasons. Oscar Cullman put forth an opposing opinion, that from New Testament times onward, word, prayers, and breaking of the bread were all one service.[32] Reginald Fuller and most contemporary scholars accept Cullman's arguments as best reflecting what we know of the practice of the early church.

The action of the liturgy of Word and Sacrament moves with integrity and grace as a unity. From beginning to end, the eucharistic liturgy is essentially of one piece. The whole liturgy forms one drama, with one essential plot, unifying the community and all of its members. The sermon or the readings or prayers are not intrusions but part of a whole. However, the sermon in particular has not been regarded in such light for a good period of Christian history.

For a long period of time, perhaps from the fifth century on in the Latin church, the sermon became increasingly disconnected from the rest of the liturgy.[33] The Lutheran reformation tried vigorously to reintegrate the two, but that effort quickly fell apart. Particularly in Protestant churches, in part because of the infrequent celebration of Communion, the sermon became a separate event, often the climax of worship. Usually such sermons were dry and intellectual arguments to convince people to do or believe the right thing. The evangelical preaching that arose in the eighteenth century in reaction to such sermons often turned into an overtly and sometimes quite dishonest effort to make people feel guilty and sinful, and therefore in need of salvation.

Not really until the biblical and liturgical revival of this century has the notion of preaching integrally connected to the liturgy returned firmly to the fore.[34] The movement to restore the interrelationship of sermon to the whole of the liturgy is also related to the contemporary effort to understand the sermon not as an artificial conceptual structure, but as a narrative art form with a plot and dramatic movement. This style of preaching intends to integrate the cognitive and affective elements of preaching, in order to address the whole person, who worships with mind and heart.

In the 1970s the study of preaching shared in some of the same conceptual revolution that affected other disciplines, with the reintegration of appreciation for the affective and emotional dimensions of human mental activity and decision-making. On a practical level, that meant a movement away from the "three point" sermon, which proposed a thesis and elucidated it with three points in more or less Aristotelian style and appealed solely to the rational, logical self. Instead, a variety of teachers of preaching started exploring narrative and story modes of preaching and the affective and imagistic dimensions of effective preaching.[35]

Eugene Lowry produced some of the consistently best writing about this new approach. In the late 1970s, he proposed that the sermon was a narrative with a plot, not a conceptual building constructed with intellectual bricks and mortar. A sermon developed organically, in time, with movement, involving people through telling them of their own human predicament and its healing in the light of the Gospel. He proposed another preaching ideal to replace the three-point thesis.

Lowry insisted that the sermon catches people in the discrepancies of the human situation—that locus of our lives where what we are and what we want to be don't match and where only the Gospel can provide resolution. He identified five stages of the plot. The first is upsetting the equilibrium, when we discover that we are caught among various goods and decisions in life and don't know how to move. The plot moves through: "2) analyzing the discrepancy; 3) disclosing the clue to resolution; 4) experiencing the gospel; and 5) anticipating the consequences."[36]

Lowry's approach to the sermon was primarily affective and directed toward transformation in Christ. It was intentionally different from the dominant approaches in the past few centuries, which assumed that the purpose of the sermon was to convince us of what we ought to do and/or believe. From this perspective, when we are convinced of the truth by Scripture and sound argument, we will believe and behave properly. Lowry, along with most contemporary teachers of homiletics, has assumed the centrality of a personal encounter with God through the Scriptures proclaimed in the liturgy. Such a meeting, and the consequent transformation through grace of our hearts as well as minds, will nurture us in the process of re-creation in Christ.

Thus the general movement of the sermon focuses and recapitulates, in its narrative, imagistic way, the drama of the eucharistic meal. In the context of the specific Eucharist of the day, with its readings, its setting, its particular congregation, the sermon also assembles and draws together the congregation, leads it deeply into an encounter with God speaking through particular Scriptures, evokes a transformation of hearts, minds, and behavior, and directs the illumined and changed congregation back toward the world in which they live.

In its particular way, the sermon articulates the movement of the Eucharist, which begins by gathering the congregation and ends sending them, confirmed in their baptismal commission, back into the world. The shape and movement of the sermon is thus integrally connected to the whole of the Eucharist and recapitulates it homiletically for a specific congregation at a specific time.

How Does the Drama Unfold?

In this first chapter I have laid out general principles about the liturgy and specific ideas about liturgy as a drama in which we are both participants and recipients. Other relevant questions include: How does the liturgy play itself out, how do we participate in it, and how does it shape our lives in the world? The next chapters will discuss these issues, looking at the character of the community assembled in particular time and place, the movement of the liturgy, how we gather, how we are nourished and transformed, and how we are again sent out into the world in mission.

2.
People, Time, and Space
The Inclusive Community

Liturgy: Who, When, and Where?

> After this I looked, and there was a great multitude that no one
> could count, from every nation, from all tribes and peoples and lan-
> guages, standing before the throne and before the Lamb.
>
> (Rev. 7:9)

Different musicians and artists have tried over the course of history
to portray the crowds from every time and place who are being drawn
into God's kingdom at the fullness of time and history. Jan Van Eyck's
great altar piece in Ghent places the Lamb on the altar in the center of
a great green plain with cities and settlements, with choirs of men and
women of all sorts gathered in praise before God. Missionary movements, interfaith dialogues, and encompassing desires to see all people
gathered in community with God have been inspired by such a vision.

Who Is in the Community? The rub comes when communities ask
who really is included, and in what sense God's invitation is universal.
Let me offer two examples. Unhappily, the saying is still far too true
that eleven o'clock on Sunday morning is the most segregated time of
the week in the United States. My own neighborhood is a good example. In the immediate area, in a borough of New York with substantial
Hispanic, Black, and Asian populations, only two of eleven churches
have significant racial integration. The others are exclusively or pre-
dominantly white. Obviously, our vision of the ideal of Christian universality and our practical application of that ideal are quite separated.

Another aspect of that same issue emerged for me at a past General
Convention of the Episcopal Church held in Indianapolis. A group of
supposedly Christian protesters carried signs and placards by the audi-
torium entrance: "Fag Tutu and Fag Spong destroying the church."
"Fags and perverts going to hell." Other slogans of the same ilk were
chanted by the protesters. These protesters were driven by a vehement
hatred of gay people, convinced that God hates them and that protesters are God's chosen instruments for driving these people out of the
church, or condemning to hell any church that would include them.

Despite the fact that the bishops named are not gay, they are tarred by the same brush of damnation these hate-filled people brandish so freely, boundlessly eager to exclude people from God's church.

All discussion of universality and inclusivity is complicated, because every community needs to have some internal standards. How can the church be the church if it includes as members people who don't want to be in the church, people who actively disbelieve in its worship and beliefs, or people who have no intention of taking the church with any seriousness at all? One of the great struggles in the church today is about the incorporation of catechesis and education into the life of the church, so that our church members become more informed and more intent believers and practitioners of the Gospel.[1]

That reality of life points us to a tension in our life and worship as a Christian community. God's saving intentions are universal, but at the same time, universal love also asks a certain kind of response. In fact, people express a variety of religious and nonreligious reactions to God's invitation. Further complicating the picture, deep in the Scriptures is found a tension between the inclusivity and universality of God's love and the conviction that God has chosen in particular the people of Israel. The inclusivity of Ruth, on the one hand, and the exclusive strictures of Ezra, on the other, testify to the struggle.

Christianity tips the balance in the Hebrew Scriptures definitively toward universality and inclusiveness (for example, John 12:32, Rom. 8). The dynamic of Christian missionary work, from the days of Acts of the Apostles on, is always toward the ends of the earth. But how is this universality to be realized? Does it demand that everyone belong to the same religious community and offer the same form of response to God's invitation? Theologians even now continue to debate universality, predestination, the salvation of non-Christians, and related issues.[2]

Even in the smallest towns, people ask about the salvation of all people and relations with those of other faiths in our community. These matters must be discussed, wrestled with, prayed about, and even from time to time preached about in the liturgy. In parish worship, the questions about universality, inclusiveness, and inclusivity all frame themselves in concrete ways around diversity within the community of faith. Is the purpose of worship to make as many people as possible feel at home, even if they do not share many Christian beliefs? How shall each community worship with many people of differing languages and cultures in their midst? Do we uphold any moral standards as intrinsic to the Christian life, or is any behavior acceptable?

My own theological judgment is that God's saving grace is universal, both in intention and in effect. This hope is an eschatological vision. I do not claim to know how God will bring about that fulfillment, only that I expect God ultimately to be "all in all" (1 Cor. 15:28). On this earth, however, I am a Christian called to be faithful to the belief and practice shaped by the community of Jesus' followers and entrusted to the church through the years. This Jesus is a universal figure of divine justice and love for all but does not demand that all people belong to the church. The church as a visible group of people finds its identity as the community that witnesses to and exists in communion with God through Jesus.

Thus the inclusiveness of the church's worship is not at root the unthinking desire to stuff every appealing thing into the liturgy in the hopes that people will enjoy it, but a ritual symbolic action both forming and expressing identity. Inclusiveness is not simply tossing everything into the liturgy. The root of the word *inclusive* is itself a helpful indicator of its meaning. The roots are Latin: "in" *in;* "claudere" *to shut up*. Inclusiveness is not, in its linguistic roots, a blanket validation of everything; rather, it begins with the notion of the borders and boundaries of a reality's identity.

Inclusiveness is the drawing of various individuals or groups into a greater whole. The expanding identity of the inclusive reality is provided by their incorporation in the community of Jesus' followers. All of the riches of different cultures, with their different political and social milieus, are called into the church, but also are to be evaluated and included or discarded in light of their integrity with the Gospel and the truth of God in Jesus.

Centuries of experience witness to the complexity, tensions, uncertainties, and compromises of human discernment, as people struggled for true inclusiveness, witnessing to God's kingdom to come. Our age is especially sensitive to these questions, perhaps because we are in such a time of transition. We can communicate with one another virtually instantaneously all over the globe, yet we are uncertain about what is constant and rooted in our identity, and how change develops in us.

Our worship shares in these tensions simply because we are alive today. We are, I believe, called by God to accept this reality as part of our vocation as Christians and to rejoice in it rather than fear it. Because the church is universal in its orientation, we can regard our struggles with diversity, inclusivity, and our identity as God's people as part of our calling to show to the world what the reign of God on earth might look like. What will it be like when all people are joined in the worship of God and community with one another?[3]

For various Christian communities in their different contexts, these responses will be different, and there are certainly many ways in which people and their cultures from our different communities can and should express authentically our common worship in various cultural forms. Each community will live and work with these questions, searching and experimenting with different customs and usages, including dance, language, vesture, and so forth. Most churches are exploring the issues involved by the inclusive expansion of their liturgical forms.[4]

In this process of growth and change, the roots of liturgy always remain in the dynamic of worship as the human expression of God's communion with us as a people. For us as Christians, our community worship is focused in the Eucharist, to which we are admitted through Baptism. We pray daily both as a community and as individuals. Such prayer is always our response to God's invitation to us and our approach to God in the name of God's whole world. The tension between the particularity of various cultural expressions and the universal sharing in the Banquet of the Lamb is a life-giving struggle, which can make the Church more honest and truthful as a worshiping community.

Perhaps an even more controversial issue is that of who can be part of the worshiping community. Probably most people would reply by asserting that anyone is welcome who repents of their sins and believes in the Lord Jesus, or who has been baptized and is in love and charity with their neighbor, or some such basic formula. Today the most divisive questions focus around sexuality. Many denominations today in the United States have focused much of their disputes about religious and cultural change and adaptation around the issue of the inclusion of gays and lesbians in the church.

How does this affect the liturgy? Some churches have excluded from communion people who have same-sex partners; others wait for such persons to publicly declare their situation before excluding them;

others do not regard it as a relevant issue; and a few have a positive and affirming stand toward gays and lesbians. Very few churches exercise the same disciplinary rigor with respect to heterosexual adultery or even child abuse. Most churches have stopped giving doctrinal tests of communicants, so that a communicant's Christology or pneumatology is not usually used as a standard of inclusion or exclusion. Very few openly raise the question of why sexual orientation and practice are so critical, rather than doctrine or other community or private ethical behaviors.

On a theoretical and a practical level, a generous catholicity always seems to me the best response to the question of who is included in the active worship life of the church. If a baptized Christian comes to worship and is not publicly making a mockery of Christian discipleship, that person is a part of the worshiping community, a forgiven sinner like the rest of us. To exclude such a person is a serious, perhaps even sinful act. A more constructive approach would be to ask about the relation of responsible sexual behavior to worship and life in the world.

Particularly where the mind of the church is not clear, for example, about homosexuality, full inclusion in the worshiping community seems most appropriate. If such behavior is contrary to our created nature, the power of the Eucharist can work its converting power. If such behavior is natural, then the church will learn from such people how to change its defective and culture-bound understandings of the Gospel and will not be guilty of the sin of driving good Christians from the community.

At the same time, the church is called to present as clearly as it can to the world and to itself the standards of the Gospel, judging and healing each and all of us. Its standards will be positive, following the Jesus who promises never to cast out those who have come to him. Inclusivity will be understood as key to transforming all people who will transform the world in Jesus' name. Worshiping communities will be strengthened by listening to each other, searching the Scripture together, learning and interpreting its heritage, and discussing today's issues and challenges. All of their prayer and reflection will focus on opening themselves responsively to God's transforming love. Inclusivity, in this ecclesial context, is not lack of standards but a life-long process of drawing all who are willing into the community, to grow in God's life and love as they are able.[5]

Time and Space in Worship. The human worshiping community does not float in an atemporal vacuum. We live in a specific time and place, in a changing physical cosmos. Our worship is shaped by the complex realities of our lives, the interconnection of past and future with their present, our sense of belonging in a specific space, and the relationship of that place to the rest of the world that we have experienced, and to that which we have heard, dreamed of, or imagined. Thus time and space are necessarily and naturally included in worship. We now turn our attention to their inclusion.

When we enter the church, a central aspect of our worship is the remembrance of a long past event, with reference to other past events, as well as to a future that is not a part of the history we study in school. The temporal web of liturgy is complex. Every act of worship commemorates the life, death, and resurrection of Jesus and is situated in and refers explicitly to the present. In addition, every liturgical activity is woven into a liturgical year, with its own rhythm of commemorations of long past events.

The church building is also involved in the rich interconnection of liturgical time and space. Each church building has signs and symbols recalling biblical, historic, and other, more recent and particular past religious events. The space itself proclaims its distinctiveness. It is similar to but not "just like home." At first glance, we see that it has seats, benches, and a table at the center. But then we notice that it has other things that either are not in most homes or are specifically designed for this place—pulpits, space for processions, special hangings and decorations, baptismal fonts, an altar-table that rarely looks like an ordinary dining room or kitchen table, and so forth. The people and leaders of worship have certain stereotyped places to fill, words and gestures that are not the words and gestures of everyday life. The space dedicated to liturgy is both related to and distanced from daily life.

Worship is, from such a perspective, a complex action. It relates our present experience of life in time and space to other dimensions of reality. Part of the joy and the frustration of worship is that it is not *just like* everything else we do. Its peculiar time and space proclaim worship's connection with and distance from the world in which we all live. Liturgical worship is an event in which we and our world consciously connect ourselves with God's eternity and the cosmic expanse of God's involvement in the world, to let ourselves be nourished and shaped by it, as well as to actively play our part in the drama of "God-with-us."

In liturgical events, time and space are of vital significance, because in them we both express our own personal and individual identity and become a self-conscious part of God's connection with the world. Thus liturgy is about ourselves and our identity as members of a human community, but, even more significant and crucial, it is also about our identity in relationship to God and to the universe through God. This identity is formed in time and space, connecting us to the heart of the universe and the infinite depths of divine life.

Sacred and Profane

One of the great scholars of the twentieth century, Mircea Eliade, explored in depth the concept of time in world religions. His descriptions offer a helpful phenomenology (theory of how we perceive religiously). He identified two modes of perceiving the world: the sacred and the profane. In the sacred mode, the person wishes to participate in the world of the divine, the sacred, which is both other than us and fascinating for us, the source of our life and reality. The profane mode of perception has been ushered in with the scientific and technological revolution. It sees all the world as one physical, scientifically measurable reality. In such a world, there is no sacred, because everything that exists can be quantified, controlled, and identified.

Eliade wrote about early religious practices, in which people recognized certain space and time as sacred, that is, time and place when the "sacred shows itself to us." What is notable about these hierophanies (manifestations of the sacred) is that the sacred, which is qualitatively different from this world, the profane world, shows itself to humanity in and through the ordinary material and events of this life. The purpose of the hierophanies is to allow humans access to the sacred in order that they may participate in its reality and connect themselves and their world to the sacred world that is the source of their life.

Profane persons regard all time and place as qualitatively the same. Being born, eating, having sexual relations, dying—all are simply biological activities with some sociological significance. The sacred as such does not exist; it is absent, nonexistent, or purely a matter of feeling.

The profane person regards the one with a sacred perspective as hopelessly outmoded, existing in an imaginary universe. The religious person is puzzled and perhaps troubled by a profane viewpoint that is perceived as a shallow and inadequate vision of the world—perhaps as one threatening the very fabric of society.[6]

In our contemporary world, Eliade perceived our technological society as caught between two visions of time, neither of which is entirely satisfactory. People feel uncomfortable with the archaic form of sacred time, with its assumption of a direct causal connection between our actions in sacred time and the divine. For example, if we offer a votive sacrifice according to the proper ritual on the correct date, our crops will certainly grow, because in response to our sacrifice God will cause them to flourish.

But a profane view, which asserts the homogeneity of the world and denies any sacred or divine reality or power in the universe, throws us into a terrifying cosmos in which we are powerless spectators, fallen into a patternless and measureless time. So terrifying, unsatisfying, and unbelievable is such a world to most people, that few individuals take such a position consistently. Amid the most modern of university students, for instance, we find enthusiastic followers of astrology and psychically powerful crystals. As the officially atheistic U.S.S.R. crumbled, people's interest in religion mushroomed.

We find such human conflict between the sacred and profane ways of viewing the world mirrored in our contemporary efforts to formulate a satisfactory interpretation of time and history. Is human (or even universal) history linear and progressive? Cyclical? Chaotic? We humans seek order and meaning and want to be participants rather than victims. But does our vision of time and history allow us to do so? Does one find a connection between God and humans, or the world and sacred reality, in individual, inward reality but not in any observable, historical sphere? Is the only hope for us to return to nonworldly divine reality and flee earthly history?[7]

The Christian vision of liturgical time offers humanity a way to reconcile our terror and hope, an approach that respects the human desire to find a divine dimension to life and recognizes the integrity of human history. In liturgical time, through the action of God's Spirit, worshipers discover between God and the world a connection that respects the world's own history and process of change, at the same time as it illumines the presence of God in and through all reality. In liturgy, according to Eliade, we enact and resymbolize the foundational realities of our faith in time and space, both because these events happened in history and because we claim that God is still active in history to redeem it in all its temporal and spatial reality.

Liturgical Time

Time, Change, and God. What is time? Since humans started asking questions, we have reflected with puzzlement on the nature of time and our relationship to it. We are born, mature, grow old, and die; the seasons pass and then recur; the planets and stars move in predictable but slightly changing cycles. How do we fit into these cosmic movements? How does God relate to the passage of time? Is God Time or Timelessness?

The Christian religious tradition has not always perceived a clear connection between time, the changing movement of the visible world, and God, who is acclaimed as unchangeable and eternal. In the *Confessions,* Augustine of Hippo mused about memory, time, creation, and God.[8] In the thirteenth century, Thomas Aquinas explored in depth the idea of God as both unmovable and prime mover and questioned whether God could still be creator if the world was without temporal beginning or end.[9] Ordinary people and scholars have shared his concerns over the centuries: How do we, in this transitory life (if we can at all), relate to God? How does God the creator—if at all—relate to our time, with its varied changes and chances? Or is God an integral part of time, subject to change as we are? Or are all of these categories inadequate and useless?

Theories of Time. Humans have always been fascinated by our experience of time. We mark the passing of days and seasons. We note to each other how quickly time flies when we are having fun; conversely, time creeps when we are in some boring or painful situation, such as sitting in the dentist's chair. Augustine of Hippo marveled about the psychological marvel of the human mind's memory, which can encompass our past and present, unifying them, imagining the future, unbound by external time and space. At the same time, so complex is time, wrote Augustine, that whenever I imagine that I am in the present, it is already past to me.[10]

Not only do we experience time, but we have also learned to measure it and reflect upon it as a reality distinguishable from ourselves. Anthony Aveni defines time from an anthropological perspective as an idea, our way of trying to put order into the world, our effort to fashion days, months, years, to give measure to what would otherwise be an undifferentiated whole. Time is also, he suggests, a reality with qualities of its own, usually conveyed in similes from our ordinary conversation, related to weather, progress, travel, and so forth. Time is interconnected with motion and change in the universe.

How do we humans connect time to change in our universe?[11] At the very beginning, recorded human efforts to measure time seemed to respond to our need to measure seasons of growth and cycles of time. When is it "time" to plant? How long is the growing "season"? When is it "harvest time"? When humans changed from being wandering tribes to becoming settled societies, they had to agree on some common measurements and possess the knowledge to grow or at least harvest crops. For these activities, a calendar of some sort was essential, one that could measure the movement of the sun and the moon. From such a beginning, with year, month, week, and day, we can see the calendar develop.[12]

As calendars were evolved in different cultures and civilizations, various cycles developed. The West, for instance, thought in centuries and millennia; the Maya had the agricultural year and the sacred cycle with the long count, with shorter and longer sacred cycles. All people developed some sort of calendar that marked time for them, with various cycles connected with crops, the heavens, and the deities. People did not want to know about time because of detached curiosity; they measured time so that they could participate in the growing of food and the ordering of life. Calendars were powerful in delivering people from being passive observers and empowered them to be participants in the recurring cycles of time.[13]

Christian Liturgical Calendar. In early religions, as we have seen, time was perceived as cyclical, and the great challenge confronting human beings was how to gain access to the divine power that governed the cycles of nature. In Jesus' own time, such a perception of time prevailed over the Greco-Roman world. Time could be "redeemed" for human beings only if cyclical or cosmic time could be tamed of its terror by human knowledge and contact with the divine powers governing the world. Festivals, patterns of celebration, decorations, symbols—all grow from this fundamental claim of various religions.[14]

The Jewish perception of history was quite different. Although Judaism possessed a religious calendar that was organized around planting and harvest festivals, the tradition's most important feast was Passover, which by later biblical times was firmly ensconced as a recollection of God's calling the people from Egypt, an event deliberately anchored in historical time and space, not *"in illo tempore."*[15] Judaism's primary loyalty was to a God whose relationship to humanity was not bound up with seasons and cosmic cycles but was anchored in human relationships to God. Agricultural and seasonal festivals in Judaism were secondary to the radical claims of Passover, which were rooted in the people's cries to God and God's deliverance of the people.

Christianity was even more overt and absolute in its rejection of cyclical and seasonal time as our connection with the sacred. For early Jewish Christians, the celebration of the Pascha, as feast of the death and resurrection of Jesus, was the great temporal celebration of the Christian community. On Sunday, the first day of the week, the death and resurrection of Jesus were commemorated. The Gentile Christians, Thomas Talley suggests, observed Sundays as the weekly festival of the resurrection of Jesus, with no continuity with the Jewish observances. Very early in its life, the church combined the traditions of the Jerusalem Jewish community with its Paschal observance and those of the Gentile communities, which observed the first day of the week, Sunday, as the Lord's day.[16] By making such a dramatic break with the surrounding pagan religious rationale of connections with natural cycles and seasons underlying contemporary calendars, the Christian community strengthened its Jewish-derived commitment to God's involvement in history.

Sunday was observed because of its historical connection with Jesus' resurrection. The day was not deemed intrinsically sacred, in the sense of lucky or unlucky, or connected with a cosmic holy pattern or eternal event. It was the human commemoration of the historic moment of our redemption. The Christian Sunday made a radical break with the Hellenistic world's calendar system of seasons and cycles. Eucharistic worship on Sunday gave the Christian community a new and quite different Sabbath. Worship made the day sacred, but the early Christians rejected the complex system of laws and observances marking this day off from all others. Sacredness was found in the midst of ordinariness.

On Sundays there were no Sabbath rules about behavior or work; only the requirement of corporate worship to remember the "death of the Lord until he come" (1 Cor. 11:26). Thus the community expressed the Lordship of the risen Jesus in time and over its fulfillment. Through eucharistic worship, they believed, those who ate and drank "worthily" were united with Jesus until his return at the consummation of time. Early Christians also connected Sunday with the eighth day of the week, the first day of creation.[17] By doing so, they connected creation and re-creation: God's creation to begin time, Jesus' resurrection to redeem time, and the return of Jesus to transform and fulfill time.

Thus Sunday liturgy recalled Christians to the holiness of every moment of the created order, as distinguished from a perspective that claimed Sunday with its special worship was holier than other days. The Apostle Paul wrote very clearly to the new Christians that times and seasons were not themselves holy; the redemptive and transforming work of Jesus was (Col. 2:8-23). We cannot overestimate the liberating effect of the radical break the early Christian community made with the notions of an intrinsically sacred calendar. The Christian's gracious relationship with God through Jesus was the source of all holiness through the Spirit of God: Everything was equally holy to the believer in the Spirit.

Because the Christians believed very strongly that God's Holy Spirit sanctifies human beings through Christ, they concluded that Christians in their lives share in some measure in God's holiness (Col. 1:6—2:17). Time is not intrinsically holy, but it can participate in God's holiness through human sharing in Christ's redeeming and sanctifying work. In this sense, all time and history have been sanctified by the re-creative and redeeming grace of Christ, because Christ is Lord of all (Acts 2:36). All time, as it is God's through Christ, is sacred; all history can be revelatory to those who see with the eyes of faith.

Thus it is not surprising that a Christian calendar emerged rather quickly in the growing community. It was not simply a counterbalance to the Jewish or Hellenistic calendars, although that element was assuredly present and was strengthened over the centuries. The liturgical year grew out of the effort to observe the central mystery of the resurrection and also celebrate it in its historical rooting, in the Jewish context of Passover and Pentecost. Christmas/Epiphany was added by the fourth century to commemorate the historical birth and manifestation of Jesus.

In this way the Christian calendar rooted the year in the crucial salvific historical events of Jesus' life: the birth-and-infancy manifestation of Jesus and his death-resurrection-ascension-sending-of-the-Spirit.[18] We are given insight into the spirit animating this development of the calendar in the work of the fourth-century bishop Cyril of Jerusalem. He was a leader in shaping a calendar and form of worship that encouraged identification with both the historical rooting and the psychological dimensions of the Christian year. Through his influence, articulating the piety of the Jerusalem church, the Christian year took on the increasing character of the believing community's accompanying Jesus through the events of his life, a kind of historical reenactment of God's work among us through Jesus.[19]

As the Christian year developed over the centuries, it grew to contain a variety of interlocked rhythms of time: the daily offices (punctuating the hours); the days of the week (Wednesday and Friday, fast days, culminating with Sunday, the great weekly festival); and seasons (Christmas/Epiphany, celebrating the Incarnation, Easter, the resurrection, and Pentecost, the coming of the Spirit to create the church). The saints' days were observed to commemorate heroic Christians who gave a moral example and connected the present generation of Christians with ages past.

The Christian calendar therefore commemorated the historically rooted "seasons" of Jesus' life and church's continuance of his mission to the world. The sanctoral cycle added the ongoing historical dimension to the familiar cycle of the events of Jesus' life, death, and resurrection. In its actual observance, the pattern of the liturgical year is more like a spiral than like the familiar repetitive pattern of the seasonally based calendars. Each year the festivals were observed, not only had the worshiping community observing the seasons grown and changed, but the calendar itself had changed, honoring new saints as a reminder of the ongoing development of the body of Christ, the community of believers.

The figure of a spiral, rather than simply a progressive line or an endlessly repetitive circle, reminds us that the Christian vision can bear a great deal of reality. The observance of the liturgical year assures us that God does not simply shoot us forward through history in uninterrupted progress, nor are we simply stuck in human history where we were two thousand years ago. We have in some ways progressed, in other ways just been moved forward, in others perhaps regressed. Nonetheless, in grace as a people we move forward, because we are drawing closer to God's fulfillment of time. History moves toward an omega point, whether or not one understands such fulfillment as Chardin has expressed it.[20]

Through our worship in liturgical time we return again and again to the roots of our life, those key events of Jesus' revealing of God to us, and we are nourished and move forward as God's people. We press on, responding to God's call to us toward the heavenly city, the fulfillment of time. Tripping, falling, rising, and responding, through our participation in liturgy, we move in our human history, from, with, and to God.

Individuals and communities also have their own ways of sharing in the Christian year, carrying on traditional observances and making efforts to find new meaning in such familiar festivals as Christmas. For each person, the calendar bears its own mix of communal event and individual adaptation. Liturgical communities and families invest the feasts with personal meaning, resonating with the depths of the human psyche. On Christmas and Easter, lights proclaim the victory of God from darkness and despair but also remind us of our own vulnerability and dependence on God. The warmth of the celebration in congregations, with hymns, familiar liturgy, and heightened community participation, strengthens the human ties as well as the often unarticulated sense of belonging to the church as the bearer of the divine to our world. When another personal milestone, such as baptism, confirmation, marriage, ordination, or funeral, is celebrated or remembered on a particular day, the individual liturgical and personal mix is even richer.

Most people feel themselves connected to the church through these great festivals, with their complex of religious and social ritual. Around these festivals, communities also create "custom-made" calendars, in which a festival (such as St. Lucy's Day) may have great importance in Sweden, for instance, and be virtually ignored in Bolivia. Individuals will also invest certain days that may or may not be specially designated in the calendar with personal significance, as with the birthday, wedding anniversary, ordination, and death dates of loved ones. Although these will never be on the calendar of the universal church or even of national churches, they are part of the rich interplay in the Christian year between individual and community in our life as members of Christ's body.

When the more radical Reformers in the sixteenth century, such as John Calvin, abolished the church year in order to return to the primitive observance of celebrating the Lord's day and no other feast, they endeavored to overthrow centuries of development in the church, as well as the natural need to connect our lives with Christ through the calendar. In the nonliturgical churches, they succeeded to a significant degree, but other "seasons," such as, in the Reformed churches, the quarterly communion and the days of preparation, took on some of the spiritual significance of Christmas and Easter.[21] By the nineteenth and twentieth centuries a vast array of "special Sundays," such as Rally Sunday, Boy Scout Sunday, and World-wide Communion Sunday, marked the calendar.

Increasingly the Reformed and Free Church traditions are now resuming the use of a lectionary and at least major Christian festivals as a reaction to the catalog of human issues and special concerns that grew up to occupy their calendars.[22] Today most Christians agree that sacred time, both in the movement of the service and in the calendar, is a vital element in connecting Christians as members of the body of Christ, and in drawing the worshiping community into its broader union with Christ and the world. There is more and more agreement that the Christian calendar appropriately focuses on the great feasts of the life, death, and resurrection of Jesus, and the coming of the Spirit.

Sacred Time in a Secular World. Contemporary Western technological culture perceives time and calendars quite differently from this older view. For the Christian this change is of vital importance. According to our current popular scientific worldview, with its roots in the eighteenth century Enlightenment, we are products of a cosmic process who watch and at best can understand what is happening to us. We have little immediate and no ultimate control in the cosmos. Present-day scientific theory disagrees about whether the universe is ordered and purposeful or the product and expression of uncertainty and chance.[23] Scientists debate about whether the universe is governed by design or chance, and what room, if any, there might be for some sort of God in these variously conceived universes. Depending on which theory of the universe and its origin one follows, God may be given no role, a limited role, or the determinative role. The average contemporary Christian, who lives in both a technological world and a religious world, will experience some dissonance, either articulate or inchoate, between the experience of liturgical time, which seeks the presence of God, and of secular time, which ignores or denies God's reality. Thus what we believe about time is profoundly important both to liturgy and to daily life.

Alan Dunstan quite rightly remarks: "What we believe about God must be the starting point for the discussion of worship . . . just as it is the starting point for most questions about the Christian faith, and indeed, about wider questions about life itself."[24] Liturgy and liturgical time are realities dependent on God; consequently, our understanding of the significance of liturgical time as rooting and grounding all of our time is directly related to our understanding of God and of God's relationship with our universe.

The root Christian notion of God and of God's relationship to the world is that God is always present and active among us. God is not a magical presence or absentee landlord; God is immediately accessible and alive among us. Aidan Kavanagh insists that the church's liturgy "transacts the church's faith in God under the real presence of God in the church and in the world."[25] The church's faith begins with its belief in God, an assumption that the world is not just plopped down into place by accident and that life is not simply "full of sound and fury, signifying nothing." Even when individually or corporately we feel distress, pain, and the personal loss of direction and meaning, we cling to the belief that God is creative power, sustaining us and concerned about us, regardless of how we may feel at the moment.

Time, for the Christian, is the measure of purposeful life, the sphere for God's involvement with us. In our worship, we draw together feelings, everyday experiences, scientific theories, and religious aspirations. Today we seek for a way we can express and experience the connectedness of past, present, and future in relationship with God.[26] Liturgy is the medium for such expression.

In worship, therefore, we seek an expression of time as the sphere of our encounter with God, not just individually but as a human community. In worship we make explicit what normally is only assumed in other contexts: God is present among us, attends to us, listens to us, communicates with us, and acts among us. Liturgical time gives form and order to our fundamental human faith.

In liturgy, time is the vehicle of creative love and redeeming grace. Bernard Iddings Bell wrote that liturgy is the central act of worship that Christians offer God through Jesus, and it is also:

> the chief channel by which has flowed into Christian people the strength which has enabled them to work in such fashion as has made the world a better place wherein to live and move and grow, in which to die without despair.[27]

Liturgy has such powerful potential because it encapsulates, reenacts, and symbolizes the whole of life in a context of gracious divine and human interaction in time and space. It is not tied to a magical view of the world, but seeks to bring the thinking, feeling, critical, and hopeful human being into contact with God. Liturgy is the great interconnection of ordinary and divine, physical and temporal, totally mundane and absolutely holy.

Liturgical time expresses this connection, whether in the first century or the late twentieth. In liturgical time we encounter God's eternity. More accurate, God's eternity encounters our time. The difference between God's eternity and our time allows God to hold all of our history, past, present, and future, in the divine present; our history thus becomes, in our act of worship, also our present. In liturgy we allow God to bring us into the interconnection between our time and God's eternity.

The central point of this connection is the Eucharist. A. G. Herbert asserted that all human history finds its meaning in the Eucharist: "If it were possible for us to comprehend its full meaning, we should see there, focused in one point, God's whole redeeming work for all mankind[sic], past, present, and future."[28] His words remind us that liturgical worship, in the Christian perspective, is a real communication between God and humanity. God's redeeming work for us is not manifest in the Eucharist just for show or pious meditation. God's eternal love encounters our time in order to reconnect us with God and with each other, in our present, but also in past and future. In liturgy, we momentarily glimpse the new creation, the whole of the heavens and the earth recreated through Christ in the Spirit.[29]

As the liturgical action unfolds, the worshiping community affirms the reality of its own life, with birth, family life, friends, achievements, tragedies, sickness, death, and the whole round of life's ordinary events. The liturgy interweaves each community's life with God's presence in the world, centered in the life of Jesus Christ, and expressed through the whole history of the old and new Israel. Through such a process of interconnection between God and the community in the liturgy, the reality of daily life, created by and directed toward God, is transformed through God's grace and perceived by us for what it truly is.

Liturgical Space

Foundations of Sacred Space. We humans are embodied creatures. Part of our historical reality is our walking, standing, talking, kneeling, singing, in this or that place. We live in a city, for instance, Iowa City, Iowa. The sidewalks have been renovated downtown, so they lie flat and aren't so buckled and cracked. The sun shines down in the heat of summer, but during the winter, evening shadows appear early and the prairie wind blows across the river, around corners, down chimneys, and rattles the stained glass in Trinity Church across the street from the library. Each of us lives in a such a place, where we feel, see, touch, and listen.

For corporate worship, we seek and make a place where our prayers and reflections can be acted out, where as a community we can receive God's word and sacrament and strengthen our bonds with one another. A place for worship is just as interconnected with our human worship as is liturgical time. Sacred space is our counterpart of sacred time. Can we pray anywhere? Yes. Are all places suitable for liturgical corporate worship? No. If we wish to encourage and nurture good liturgy, we must understand the dynamics of sacred space.

In the Four Quartets, Eliot wrote of sacred space in "Little Gidding":

> If you came at night like a broken king,
> If you came by day not knowing what you came for,
> It would be the same.
>
> . . .
>
> You are here to kneel
> Where prayer has been valid.[30]

Human beings seem to have a fundamental instinct, as basic as the desire to mark time or to communicate with each other, to respect sacred spaces. Eliot articulates the essence of the experience of sacred space, that we sense places that have been places of prayer for long periods to be "hallowed." God and humanity have communicated in this physical place, and the purpose of that place is to encourage and nurture such communication.

Mircea Eliade wrote at great length of the primordial human experience of sacred space. He suggested that humans never regard all space as the same, just as we differentiate times. Sacred space, as compared to profane, homogeneous space, is a place of hierophany, a connecting point between the divine and the world. In sacred places, the sacred "irrupts" and emerges into human life, to communicate and reveal the divine to humanity. Such space, Eliade asserts, is continuous with ordinary space—it is like other space; it has a door for entrances and exits— and at the same time, it is a place where either the divine has made itself known, or a manifestation of the sacred has been "provoked."[31]

Christian Sacred Space. Temples and holy places are part of every religion, whether the place be one set aside for worship by the community, one where the deity has manifested itself, or any place that is made holy through the encounter of God and the believer. In the Christian tradition, the primary place of worship is the Christian her- or himself (1 Cor. 3:16-17). The Holy Spirit dwells in the believer through Baptism. The author of Acts shows Stephen, in his sermon before the Sanhedrin, uttering a strong version of the radical Christian critique of Jewish Temple worship: "God does not dwell in temples made by hands" (Acts 7:48).

Such a radical questioning of sacred places is rooted in the prophetic strain of the Hebrew Bible. Isaiah, Jeremiah, Amos, and others vigorously attack the claim that any place is holy just because it is designated as holy. God is everywhere; holiness is present when people receive and live by God's law and pray to the God whom they obey (for example, the Temple sermon in Jeremiah 7). The prophets' objection to sacred places is directed not at the use of particular places for worship, but at the substitution of form for authentic worship in heart and deed. Without denying that God's place of worship, the temple, was holy, the prophets added two ingredients to holiness of place: human moral response to God's self-revelation, and the possibility of universal revelation of God through human seeking of God (Micah 1:11). This prophetic relationship to sacred space was characteristic of Jesus and his disciples.

It appears that although the early Christians' theology was rooted in this prophetic-Pauline vision of the believer as the temple of the Holy Spirit, the early Christians, when it was practically possible, also had holy places. Tombs of martyrs, church buildings, places connected with God's communication with humanity were holy places for the Christians before Constantine.[32] At the same time that they seemed to prefer to have special designated places of worship, Christians affirmed a religious insistence that the church was the assembly of the believers; the church building could be one used for the occasion or built for that purpose.[33]

After Constantine's recognition of Christianity, church architecture flourished, and church buildings were constructed all over the empire. Alexander Schmemann regards this period as a shift from a focus on the church as the meeting place for the Christian assembly to a focus on the church as a place holy in itself.[34] Most Christians probably held to the belief that the church was the assembly of believers and the worship by the assembly, focused around the altar-table, was the holy event. At the same time, the worship by the community became increasingly localized in one place, which was then given an aura of holiness. The new connection of altar, relics, and tombs of the saints and holy ones contributed to the growing understanding of the church as a place hallowed by the altar and the saints, a perpetual place of connection of the divine and human, heaven and earth.[35]

Even if one does not regard the shift in the Middle Ages as a complete change from one view of the church building to another, at the very least one must admit a major change in emphasis. The church soon became a shrine, a place of pilgrimage, considered holy in and of itself, as well as a place where the community of the faithful came to assemble before God. During the Middle Ages, both in East and West, the church building increasingly was regarded as sacred space.[36]

In the European Middle Ages, architectural devices proliferated to keep ordinary people at a distance and set off the most sacred space in the church—for example, rood screens, choir stalls, altars pushed to the wall. The Reformers tried various approaches to draw clergy and congregation together and to return to the earlier notion of the church building as the assembly of the faithful, hallowed by worship, not in and of itself holy through relics, altars, and so forth. Over the next centuries, while the Roman Catholic tradition retained a fundamentally medieval notion of sacred space, other Western traditions attempted different approaches to the assembly for worship, such as the Enlightenment preaching church, meeting houses, a previously constructed sanctuary area rearranged to put altar and pulpit in an equal balance. The Gothic revival of the nineteenth century saw an effort in various traditions to adapt the medieval style to various, and sometimes unsuitable, religious styles. More contemporary religious architecture endeavors to combine function and theological vision in the building and its arrangements. The modern liturgical revival has produced churches whose primary goal is to provide an environment that facilitates community worship.[37]

The place of the altar, the lecterns, use of rails, relation of the congregation to the place of celebration, places of entrance and exit—all express visually what the community feels and believes about its participation in its own worship and its willingness to assume its place as a responsible worshiping community. The process of major or minor church renovation may bring to the fore the congregation's feelings about worship. The challenge then becomes the congregation's readiness to transform itself and to incorporate others into its life of worship.

When, for instance, in the renovations of a long, narrow neo-Gothic parish church, the pews were taken out, the congregation was seated in movable cathedral chairs, which allowed substantial freedom in placing the congregation near the altar. Instead of staying around the altar, people grabbed their chairs and hung as far back as possible. Strangers could be identified by how close they sat and stood near the altar. Obviously, the old architecture had been modified, but medieval patterns of space usage still governed people's instincts.

Even in churches unchanged from their older origins, use of seasonal decoration and people's eagerness to be near other members of the worshiping community and move about during appropriate parts of the liturgy can make the space suitable for contemporary worship. In a multilingual or multicultural situation, pictures or decoration can create a welcoming atmosphere for the congregation. Absence of clutter and as open a space for worship as possible can invite worship, even if congregations cannot invest significant time or money into preparation of the church for congregational worship.

Sometimes as a matter of choice and on other occasions because of necessity, many congregations will allow their liturgical space to be used for other purposes. In some places, the space will be built for just such multipurpose usage; in other situations the space will simply be appropriate for other usage. It seems right, proper, and traditional that church space be used for other purposes—plays, concerts, meetings, and so forth. At the same time, users of the space for those other purposes also need to be sensitive to the primary raison d'être of the space—worship. Each congregation will want to devise ways to ensure that its space is always respected and especially that its sacred objects, such as altars, are carefully protected from misuse. The worshiping congregation must be the chief actor in setting the appropriate terms for its sharing of space.

The form of our church and our use of space in worship are vital components of our developing liturgy.[38] As James White reminds his readers, the Christian tradition takes the incarnation very seriously. The event of our redemption takes place in time and space, and the place where holy events have occurred is a "bearer of meaning" for us.[39] Because the event of redemption is renewed in worship and the Christian assembly is nurtured and restored through its participation in the saving event of redemption, the space where the community worships always both reflects and shapes our life with God.

Processions, recessionals, offertory processions, when and where we stand, sit, or kneel, our interactions during the liturgy, our relationship to the altar and pulpit—all express our identity and reinforce or conflict with what we want to be as a parish community. Part of a community's self-awareness and education is bound up with its willingness to worship in its space in flexible and thoughtful ways. At the same time, the use of space also anchors a community in its traditions and offers the support of continuing patterns of use. Change and stability in ways of worshiping in liturgical space always dance in delicate balance.

The space in which we worship is formative to our identity because it gives three-dimensional expression to our belief that Jesus became incarnate for us, and all of our space is made holy through the incarnation. Furthermore, it is a place where God's grace has been manifest, received, and responded to. The church building is an expression and intensification of the holiness of God expressed in the whole created and redeemed universe. It is also a place where the Christian community gives intentional and self-conscious utterance and active articulation to its role in God's redemptive activity in the world.

An additional dimension of contemporary church architecture is our recognition that, because it expresses our faith in the saving action of our incarnate Redeemer, the building is a sign of the unity of heaven and earth, divine and human in Christ. Worship space expresses what is and what is in process of becoming through the grace of God. In this sense, our liturgical space is cosmic, a symbol of the eternal messianic banquet. The Eastern Churches have always retained this theological vision, even when the infrequent communion of the laity did not support the symbolism well. The church, with its liturgical action, is the place where we participate here and now in the unity of all creation in God. This unity is present through the liturgy and will be made perfect by God in all creation at the end of time.[40]

As we Western Christians reincorporate this dimension to our incarnational faith, we are reminded by attention to time and space that our worship is corporate in the widest possible sense, with and on behalf of the whole cosmos. At the Sanctus, we pray with saints and angels and all the hosts of heaven and cry out with all creation. Increasingly, we Christians accept that our liturgy expresses the intrinsic interconnection of the whole world with God. Thus our worship and its space need to express both God's order of creation and redemption in the universe now and our hope for our fulfillment to come. We want our church buildings, their furnishings, and our worship to express the liturgy of the cosmic community in which we participate.

3.
The Word and the World
God's People at Worship and Work

Ordinarily I avoid children's sermons like the plague. In my experience, they are either thinly disguised appeals to the adults or feeble church versions of show-and-tell, desperately trying to be cute. However, on the First Sunday after Easter, our eucharistic celebration was one in which the children participated in various lay leadership roles of the liturgy. Thus it seemed fitting and proper to eat my words about children's sermons.

So I plunged into the fray and planned my "children's sermon" for everyone assembled that day. Because we were in the Easter season (and I knew better than to try publicly to discuss the resurrection with *our* marvelously normal and unpredictable children), I decided to talk about Baptism with them.

That Sunday we gathered by the font at the back of the church, inside the doors but behind the pews. The children all stood around or sat on the floor, as we began our conversation about Baptism. Being in a mood of Easter optimism, I asked a wide-open question. "Why is the font right here by the door?" Up popped a little hand. "So when we come in, we can remember we are God's children, and when we go out, we can remember how we are supposed to act."

I decided to stop there. The congregation was astonished at the truth that had tumbled out of "the mouth of babes." None of us will ever see our parish's baptismal font in the same light again. Furthermore, we will never dare disconnect Baptism from our coming together to celebrate the Eucharist and going out again at our dismissal. Our four-year-old baptized theologian reminded us all of what connects Baptism and Eucharist with our identity as Christians in the world.

Gathering the Baptized

In the early days of the church's existence, gathering together was an important activity in and of itself. Not everyone was a Christian or even well-disposed toward Christians. When the door opened to admit people to the Eucharist, the community was vitally interested to see who came in. Would Sarah and Samuel sustain their commitment to Jesus as Messiah? Could Cornelia extract herself from Tertius's household and join the other Christians at Suplitia and Theodore's home? Would Simplicius forever waver in his desire to live as a faithful baptized Christian? Would those two slaves and one shopkeeper preparing to accept Baptism in the name of Jesus persevere? Instead of known and trusted friends, would soldiers instead arrive, heralding persecution and perhaps death?

Today, for most of us in North America, our liturgical gathering is different. Persecutions and discrimination have been and continue to be part of the global Christian experience. However, the religious context in which we worship is more likely to be that of pluralism, not persecution. Christendom is dead. We live in a world in which it is increasingly unlikely that the majority of people in any country will actively practice Christianity or profess and live by its values.

Modern communication and transportation have allowed different groups of people to disperse all over the globe. People from other nations, worshipers of Kali or followers of Islam, move to North and South America. Much more than in earlier centuries, Christians are everywhere, even where they are only a handful in cultures espousing different religious or other faiths. Almost nowhere is the religious picture homogeneous. Pluralism is becoming our normal way of life all over the globe.

In addition, in the last decade or so, Americans have begun to live in a social world that Europeans have known for some time. Believing and practicing Christians have become a minority in the lands they had once considered their own. The percentage of people for whom religion is very important seems constantly on the decline. At the least, one can no longer assume that baptism and some vague connections with the church are a part of everyone's upbringing. The phenomenon of "secularism" describes an increasing number of Americans.

To be a baptized and committed Christian is no longer simply accepted as part of the setting of our society. Even though the number of people attending church or synagogue weekly does not seem to have changed substantially since before the 1940s, this last decade has seen a noticeable increase in the number of people who identify themselves as "secularists," or as "unaffiliated with any religious organization."[1] If we take secularism in the sense of unaffiliated as a part of the religious picture, they are the proportionately fastest-growing group. Their numbers are drawn mostly from those who in a previous generation would have retained a merely nominal membership in church or synagogue. Now they have rejected that option and disassociate themselves from organized religion.

If we wished, we could spend a great deal of time exploring why these people do not come to church and what we might do to gain them back, if that is possible.[2] That is not my purpose or intention here. Instead, I wish only to draw our attention to a reality that the Christian community in North America has not had to take seriously before. The gathering of the worshiping community is not a mere continuation of people's outside activity or even of their community. Even in the closest knit and most homogeneous areas, Sunday Eucharist is not the gentry at worship or even "the Republican [or, in some areas, the Democratic] Party at prayer." The Christian community constitutes itself quite differently.

In part, this is because, despite the somewhat frantic rhetoric of religious fundamentalists, we do not live in a Christian country, even though our dominant culture has been shaped by some of the Bible's chief values, such as justice and the value of the individual. Important as those shared values are, even they have become distorted in the culture and in their cultural context seem removed from their original significance in Biblical religion. For instance, the biblically rooted assertion of the value of each unique person has become distorted into a rampant individualism that threatens the corporate character of even our religion itself.[3]

Our liturgies, to be truly the work of the people, must take account of the countercultural dimension of religious commitment and Christian belief and practice. We should not underestimate people's experience that our common social fabric is pluralistic and secular. Even when religion is valued highly, as in the United States, the cultural consensus is that religion is a matter of individual choice and not to be forced or perhaps even shared with another.

Small wonder that the identification between shared civic values and religious values is no longer even an ideal. "Civil religion" is dying and perhaps dead as an ideal. Thus we may be sure that the liturgical gathering of the faithful is an important public action, both for the individual and for the community. The person who shares in the liturgy roots her- or himself in community, which will offer life and hope but which may also pull in quite different directions from their friends' and neighbors' practices and beliefs. One who enters the church to worship expresses a commitment that is no longer simply an extension of the culture's values.

Thus the church is the home of those who hear the call of Jesus to them not primarily from cultural expectations but from commitment to the faith of the apostles. We are growing into a church that in fact no longer can assume itself to be an automatic element of any particular culture. The church must root itself not only theologically but practically in God's call to all humanity. "Behold, when I am lifted up from the earth, I will draw all to myself" (John 12:32). The church is God's people called from God's whole earth. Today we are especially challenged to live that universality in our worship.

Liturgical Greeting and Gathering

Entrance into the church for worship is an act of commitment and faith. Our liturgies themselves will be more authentic and faithful when they proclaim the church's recognition of our efforts to live and express our faith, and when they offer believers an opportunity to proclaim their own belonging to the community of faith. To worship is to express our most fundamental selves as "buried therefore with him by baptism into death, so that as Christ was raised from the dead by the glory of the Father, we might walk in newness of life" (Rom. 6:4; cf. 1 Cor. 11, 12).

Today we in our churches need to remember that the Greeting, with its hymn, acclamation, and whatever prayer introduces the liturgy, marks a vital moment of commitment for our communities. People enter the assembly from a world in which they may well be oddities as believing and practicing Christians, into a community in which Christ is the great common bond holding all together. Our worship needs to express our identity as a community baptized into a common life in Christ even to the curious or friendly nonbeliever who joins us.

Gathering and Passageway. Most Christian traditions have chosen to place the baptismal font by the entrance to the church, either in a separate building or in a special section by the door, called the baptistery.

This placement graphically marks, as my four-year-old theologian expressed, the special character of our coming in and our going out. We are made God's people through our baptism. We gather together in our community's worship because we want and need to be recalled to our true identity, to pray for our world, to be nourished in God's life, and then to be sent out again to live as God's people in the world. The font is the symbol of our identity as God's people in the world, citizens both of earth and of heaven, our lives the self-conscious interconnection of the world with God.[4]

Both in planning liturgy and in the act of worship, we should constantly remind ourselves that people come to worship God rooted in earth and stretching to the infinite. Humanity's special responsibility is to utter the cry of praise of all creation, to pray on behalf of all the universe.[5] We therefore need an act of gathering and naming ourselves as Christians who pray on behalf of and for the entire world. This gathering expresses the connection between God and God's world, as well as our brokenness and our disconnection. We celebrate the joys of life, but in the struggles of our daily life we feel ourselves tossed and pulled between the goodness of our earth and the pain of hatred, death, remorse, greed, and all the other ills we share. In our gathering, we articulate the joys and the distress of all creation, as we share together a common life God has given us.

Mircea Eliade offered one model of humanity connecting the visible universe and the realm of the sacred. He described the boundaries between the sacred and the profane world and the human desire both for a sacred space set aside for our communication with the sacred and for the sanctification of all life. He explored liminality, the importance of the door, the place where the seeker for the holy moves between the sacred and the world, and the rituals connected with this door.[6] The door (sometimes, depending on context, the ladder or bridge) is a place of passage between the earth, the sacred above, and, in some situations, the underworld.

The gathering of the community is always a kind of passage in which the Christian community comes together from the dispersed ordinary world of family and friends, work and play, as its representatives and denizens, into the self-conscious and intentional meeting place of the world and God's eternity. Liturgical community enters worship for one clear, shared purpose, no matter how many other "mixed" motives individuals may harbor. The community prays for God's justice and love, the putting of the world to rights with itself and God present in it.[7]

In the Lord's Prayer, we ask that "God's will be done on earth as in heaven." Thus we utter our conviction that God's realm is already present in creation but not in its fullness. As we gather we express our root conviction that as God's priestly people we exist in the good but sinful world of everyday, and we also reach into the wholeness of God's life with us in what we call the eternal, heavenly realm. To live fully in both realms (or both dimensions) of God's realm is difficult, because we tend either to get bogged down in our present circumstances or to flee into a fantasy heaven disconnected from God's real world. God's people require a time of gathering to bring themselves to awareness of who they are and of God's calling to them.

Liturgical Assembly and Christian Identity

Human beings crave identity. We all want to belong to a greater group or power than our own selves. We want a name, we wish to be part of a family, and we will seek a substitute if our own is inadequate. We wrestle with those who exclude us from sharing a desirable identity to which we believe we have a right. At the same time, especially in contemporary industrialized societies, we want our "own" identity, and freedom and self-determination are vitally important ideas for people.

The rapidly changing political scene and shifting national borders of recent times have radically shaken people's sense of secure identity. These events have intensified the already existing human desires for personal autonomy and self-determination as a part of a community. This complex search for identity, which can take many different forms, is one of the key themes of contemporary culture. It is also a crucial dimension of people's expectations and needs from liturgy, especially of our gathering and greeting each other as Christians in Christ's name.[8]

As we gather for Eucharist, we want on the one hand to profess our unity in Christ, a communion of the most diverse and heterogeneous folk imaginable, joined in love of God through Christ, interconnected by bonds of love, mutual respect and service, and a ministry of preaching and living the Good News in the world, laboring for God's reign on earth. On the other hand, we hold as precious our diversity and personal value before God, as individuals and as cultures. With distress we contemplate past and present efforts to equate unity with uniformity, assumptions that to become Christian was to assume a specific set of European cultural values and practices. With equal anxiety we fear an excess valuing of individuality and difference, which fractures common life and values and absolutizes uniqueness as a value in and for itself.

This struggle is central to our time; thus we ought not to be surprised that our worship reflects our concerns. None of us have all the answers or are always certain just how to discover and express our identity in specific situations. As Christians, however, we try to hang onto both values—community and individuality. Cultures will articulate this mix differently, but no one is free to omit or suppress one or the other dimension. A Christian is equally distressed by the repression of freedom in China symbolized by Tiananmin Square and by the rampant spirit of NIMBY ("not in my back yard"), which prevents us from sharing woes and risks, as well as prosperity and advantages.

In the *Paradiso* of Dante's *Divine Comedy,* we see a poetic vision of creation worshiping God. In the emporium, as Dante looks into Beatrice's eyes, he sees God as a dazzling point of light encircled by the nine rings that are the choirs of angels. In the center is the great celestial rose, in which all the varied individuals are united as one in the divine unity-in-trinity.[9] In his day, Dante expressed an order of unity in God combined with diversity of many different people from various times and places. Today we might express this vision differently. Nonetheless, the same values are involved. People entering a church to worship see a reflection of the Gospel only if unity in God's love and a rainbow of different human persons are actively included. What vision guides us?

The liturgy does not simply reflect human diversity; it creates communion out of our diversity. Christian community is a gathering of not only like-minded but also diverse people, joined by an exalted purpose. We are God's people, the body of Christ. We do not make our community to our taste and through our efforts; God through Jesus Christ in the Spirit makes us one. John A. T. Robinson, quoting John Wesley, wrote, "The Gospel of Christ knows of no religion but social;

no holiness but social holiness."[10] Of equal importance, Robinson continues, is the truth that Christian community is made through one particular kind of unity, our communion with God.

In the New Testament, Robinson notes, the Greek word *koinonia,* which we translate as *community,* refers primarily not to our community with each other, but to our communion with God, Christ, or Spirit. Our communion with each other grows from our communion with God.[11] The center and source of our interconnection with each other, we might otherwise phrase it, is with God. Our gathering as Christians expresses our joy in our life with God and in God with each other. In a world in which our human community seems fragile and vulnerable and social and political systems that ruled for decades fade overnight, as in the former Soviet Union, we are well advised to remind ourselves when we gather that we come together only because God has created and invites us to be together.

Through God's sharing of life with us, through forgiveness and love, we have received and continue to experience a love and peace (shalom) that surpass our understanding and our human capabilities. Our koinonia is God's gift that we receive, not our achievement. Our efforts bear fruit because God is in us and with us. The metaphor "body of Christ" expresses the intimacy of God's life in us, and the closeness that this life creates among us in our interrelationships with one another and with the world.[12]

The Word of God: Uttering the Dialogue

How do we act out such communion in our corporate worship? The structure of the first half of the Eucharistic liturgy, from the Greeting up to the Offertory, which begins the Communion, is a dialogue between God and the congregation. It consists of community assembly, prayer of praise, confession, intercession, and hearing of and responding to the Scriptures.

Gregory Dix, in his enormously influential analysis, asserts that the first part of our eucharistic liturgy, the synaxis, is derived from synagogue worship.[13] Scholars today would cast doubt on the sort of rigid and absolute division between synaxis and anaphora of the Eucharist that he proposed, and also on the certainty that the first part of the liturgy is rooted only in the synagogue worship and not in other Jewish worship.[14] But the main lines of the structure he sketches and the Jewish roots of the whole eucharistic liturgy point us clearly and directly to the lively interaction between God and the congregation through prayer and reading.

Dix suggests these elements of the early church's synaxis:

1. Opening greeting by the Officiant and the reply of the church.
2. Lesson.
3. Psalmody.
4. Lesson (or Lessons, separated by Psalmody).
5. Sermon.
6. Dismissal of those who did not belong to the church.
7. Prayers.
8. Dismissal of the church.[15]

Even if we are not so confident of each of the elements or its precise place as was Dom Gregory, he quite rightly prods us to recognize that the first half of the eucharistic liturgy is a dialogue, which begins with the initial greeting and then continues with listening to the Scripture and responding by the congregation in psalmody, sermon (by the president of the assembly), and prayers.

All liturgies of the Word express this dialogical quality, the alternation of listening and responding to God's word expressed in the Scriptures. The more plainly and clearly this dialogical character expresses itself, the more aware and devout the congregation's own participation may become. In this part of the liturgy, everything relates to our receiving and responding to the Word.

In my own exposition, I have chosen not to go through the liturgy step by step, but to identify the elements of each major aspect: the greeting (treated separately simply because it is so important and so often ignored or downplayed), hearing the Scriptures, and responding in prayer.

The Gathering and Greeting. Today at a Sunday service, the liturgy almost always begins with a song or hymn. Originally the music was a way of covering the movement of the clergy and altar ministers to the altar. Although it normally still serves that function, for the congregation it is primarily a moment of transition into worship. Members of the congregation, with all their varied occupations, of many ages, tastes, abilities, family interconnections, hopes, fears, and desires for the world in which they live, approach God's altar. The hymn is generally the first corporately uttered expression linking the people and their world(s) with God and God's redeeming and transforming grace.

Thus the hymn and words of greeting express the people's entrance into God's world, which is present among us and yet not dwelling in its fullness. We are one through Baptism, but not yet one in the immeasurable realities of everyday life. We are diverse but do not yet realize the fullness of the possibilities God offers us in creation. The hymn and greeting acknowledge that the congregation is and is becoming a different community, which is not coextensive with their secular community and may in fact be quite distinct from their neighborhood in the community. Thus from the beginning, our prayer nurtures through God's grace our life as God's people, "gathered from all over the earth into your realm."[16]

Hymn and greeting always thus articulate God's name, and all the presiders and the congregation greet one another to acknowledge again their relationship as a worshiping community. For example, in the Roman Catholic eucharistic liturgy, after the Entrance Song, the priest makes the sign of the cross, "In the name of the Father and of the Son and of the Holy Spirit." To which the people respond, "Amen." Then the priest exchanges greetings with the people, in the name of the Triune God. The Presbyterian Worship Book even calls the whole first part of the service *Assemble in God's Name,* including the gathering of the people, call to worship, hymn of praise, pardon or spiritual confession and pardon, act of praise, and the peace. For their ordinary greeting, to mark the Christian assembly as God's people, the Episcopal church has taken the greeting from the liturgy of John Chrysostom:

> *Celebrant:* Blessed be God, Father, Son, and Holy Spirit.
> *People:* And blessed be his kingdom now and forever. Amen.

The liturgical greeting functions as both a summons and an affirmation, calling the people to worship, acknowledging them in their role, and naming this community as God's community, serving God's reign in the world. Craig D. Erickson remarked, "The Opening Dialogue ought to be one that naturally engages the soul."[17] Theologically, liturgically, pastorally, psychologically, the moment of assembly and greeting is crucial. This moment must be planned and carried out with great care, so that people feel themselves invited to and included in the community. At the same time, the whole tenor of all the words, music, and gestures must proclaim that the gathering community draws together in the name of God, and for the service of God and God's realm on earth.

Thus the tone of the gathering greeting may and will vary depending on the season or other specific reason for worship, but it should be sure, clear, simple, and familiar. New hymns and lengthy prayers have their place, but not here. The gathering and any initial prayers ought to be as familiar as the "I haven't seen you in ages" of a family gathering.

Once we have assembled as the people of God, we can then pray and listen to God's word proclaimed to us. Our identity reasserted, we begin to listen to and reflect on our family's story and our present lives, and to speak with the God who brought us together for our sakes and for the good of the whole world.[18]

Hearing the Word. We are drawn together as Christians with a common family story. From all different nations, tongues, and family conditions, in addition to our personal, community, and national histories, we share a story together. The Scriptures are a variegated testimony to God's action in the world: creation; the calling of a people to whom God reveals the divine life and purpose; the reactions for good and for ill of that people; the life, death, and resurrection of Jesus; the outpouring of God's Spirit in human history and the birth of the Jesus movement and the church that grew from it.

In this story, we believe that God communicates with us. Revelation is a complex question with which scholars wrestle and ordinary mortals struggle.[19] For the worshiper, the root meaning of revelation is probably the most essential: God is; God, who is greater than creation, cares about the creation and about humanity; God becomes involved in our world's history in order to communicate not just information but an offer of a corporate and personal relationship with humans. The claim of a religion of revelation is that God really is truly made known through the Scriptures as a part of a living faith in which God is involved with and available to the community and the individual.

Judaism and Christianity both claim to be religions of revelation, and both have recorded what they consider to be the basic family story of their revelation. In the general consensus of the Christian tradition, there is broad agreement that our Scriptures are both God's word and human words. That is, God is really made known to us, but a lot of human material is also present in the Scriptures. It is not all transparent to God and God's intentions for humanity; some parts may be clear illustrations of human sin, whereas others may be reflective of various sinful social structures, such as patriarchal forms of oppression or slave-owning, which were simply assumed as part of the world when the revelation was written down.[20]

Our gathering always involves us in a struggle to connect our present life with the ancient Scriptures. Phyllis Trible suggests that there is an interpretive clue in the text itself, about God's self-revelation. If we attend to this clue, we discover both the dynamic of God's revelation, a critique of the human and sometimes obscuring elements of the story, and the place where Scripture dialogues with us today.[21] The primary issue in worship is that both in our listening and in our spoken words of song, prayer, and preaching, we acknowledge that the real God is revealed to us in Scripture and that every word in Scripture is not revelatory of God in any direct sense.

Family stories can serve as good analogues for us. They all contain some element of truth and tell us about the family. They also, the deeper and truer they are, testify to human sin and greed, lust and anger, as well as to love and compassion, faithfulness and justice. Some of our family stories we delight to tell; others cause us grief or shame. As we mature, we are able to see many threads weaving in and out of the stories and to discern what is the good of our family saga, the testimony to the greatness of the human spirit, in which we take pride and which inspires us.

The Scriptures are much more than just another family story, we profess, because through them and in them we hear and see God communicating with us. The Scripture itself makes that claim quite clearly. However, we need a principle of interpretation akin to the one I suggested previously, to allow us a prayerful encounter with the Scriptures, in order that we may respond to the story and make it our own.

Our preaching, rooted in the Scriptures, forms and feeds our identity as Christians, directs us to the centrality of our life with God, provides a core for our education, connects our life and our faith explicitly with the life of the community, offers us hope for the present and the future, and guides us in developing values for a truly Christian life.

Lectionary. In our worship the church does not simply throw the Scriptures at us, whole cloth, and let us take up the book and sink under the weight of the whole expanse of two thousand years. Following the practice of Jewish worship, one, two, or three selections of Scripture are appointed to be read in Christian eucharistic worship. Lectionaries, which appoint certain lessons to be read on various days, quickly replaced an earlier practice of a *lectio continua* limited by time and the inclination of the presider.[22]

Even churches that have historically rejected set liturgies today are making use of lectionaries, perhaps in recognition that in the absence of a common lectionary, the preacher frequently simply substitutes his or her own personal lectionary, albeit without as much planning as has produced denominational or interdenominational lectionaries. The next chapter, devoted to preaching, will explore more about the use of the lectionary in the Eucharist, as an orderly reading and interpreting of Scripture, seeking God's word today through Scripture's words bearing grace to us.

The great advantage of the lectionary for public worship is that it offers the community maximum exposure to the story of God's involvement with the world.[23] Through its selections of readings for the congregation's hearing and the juxtapositions of readings, the church already exercises some judgment about where and how God is revealed to us in the Scripture.

In the most recent lectionaries there are three readings for Sundays and great feasts, returning to a happier and more ancient custom of the church than the mere epistle and gospel. The first reading is from the Hebrew Bible, reminding us that we are inheritors of the revelation God gave to the Jewish people. We believe ourselves to be their brothers and sisters, even though now we are separated by a serious difference about God's self-expression in Jesus Christ. Nonetheless, our spiritual roots are in Judaism, and we worship the God of Abraham, Isaac, and Jacob, the God of Sarah, Rebecca, and Rachel.

The Psalm in the liturgy that follows the Old Testament reading and may also follow the New Testament reading is not a reading to which the congregation listens passively, but one it uses actively to praise God. Through this use of Scripture, the community affirms its belief Scriptural revelation by using the words of Scripture themselves to praise God actively. The tone of the prayer draws from the previous

reading, so that the community expresses its response to the reading
in Scriptural, liturgical words. Because the words of the Psalms derive
from corporate worship, the church from the very beginning has
employed the Psalms for the congregation's active expression of its
faith.

Two New Testament readings ordinarily are proclaimed in the
Eucharist: one from the Gospels and one from the rest of the New Testament, not only from the Epistles. One reading tells an episode from
the life of Jesus, and the other how belief in his revelation shaped the
early church. The readings are not in chronological order, however.
The Gospel is the third and last Biblical reading, thus by its place as
well as content testifying that the eucharistic liturgy expresses the
"saving work of Christ."[24]

The community responds to the readings from the Scripture first
and primarily by listening to them. Thus it is important that liturgical readers receive training about pronunciation, volume, and other
important elements of public reading. The people need to hear the
reading, to experience it proclaimed in a manner worthy of grace bearing words. Readers have a crucial role in opening the Scriptures to the
congregation.

The community also needs to understand what they are hearing.
Knowledge of the Bible cannot be presumed. Lifelong Christian education is essential nourishment for our worship. Those who are more
knowledgeable need to be encouraged to continue their efforts and to
"talk it up" with other members of the congregation. We all would
profit by much more sharing of what we know and eager investiga-
tion of the stories of our past that we do not know or understand.[25]
The whole church suffers through our ignorance and lack of appreciation of the depth and breadth of our own family story. Meaningful
participation in the Eucharist requires that we root ourselves firmly
in the Scriptures. That process requires informed, active, and attentive listening.

But we cannot assimilate the revelatory story of Scripture only
through knowledge, though we can do very little without it. Henry
Mitchell speaks words directed at the preacher but intended for all
believing Christians: "The story must be internalized in the preacher,
peopled by characters he has known for years and for whom he has
such deep feelings that he can authentically recreate the action and

communicate the experience."[26] How can we so assimilate the Scriptures into ourselves? Grace, knowledge, and prayer.

Grace and knowledge have been spoken about, but prayer is the vital link connecting Scripture, the whole Eucharist, and the world. Eucharist is prayer, and the Scripture can be prayer and, as with the Psalms, sometimes directly is. I mean only that none of us comes to the Eucharist tabula rasa. We come formed, shaped, prepared, an involved member of the community, or we may arrive at the Eucharist ignorant, careless, and uninvolved. God's grace includes us all, just as a family will include its less savory or more peripheral members. Nonetheless, to be lively and connected members of the body of Christ, we need the nurture of personal encounter with Scripture through prayer.

Public and private reading, hearing, and reflecting are essential in assimilating our story, in allowing God to open our minds and hearts so that God may be revealed to us.[27] Our heads alone give us the sort of personal connection that enables us to feel that we have known the people of the Bible for years or that God is a living reality for us. Our imaginations, our wills, our feelings also are included in our prayer. Only this fully human and interconnected personal prayer is living and true prayer and provides us nurture for our most complete participation in the community Eucharist.[28] Such private prayer is an essential animating dimension of our liturgical prayer.

Prayer. The prayer offered during the first part of the eucharistic liturgy in response to our hearing of God's word in the Scriptures takes many forms: collects, corporate prayers and hymns of praise, times of silence, the people's prayers of intercession, litanies, and the creed. Depending on the particular tradition, the precise form or placement may vary somewhat. But whatever form the prayer takes, its purpose is to utter our response to God's self-giving, which is articulated most centrally in the Scriptures proclaimed to the congregation.

Silence. Often neglected, but receiving more attention in our noisy and busy communities, is the importance of silence in the liturgy. Perhaps in less mechanized or industrialized times, silence could be assumed. Today, however, for most people there is very little silence. Even for those who live in quiet places or in the country, radios or portable stereos incessantly accompany people. True silence is hard to find.

The value of silence is not simply the absence of noise, although that may well be valuable. Silence is an invitation to recollect ourselves, to make contact with God and with the deep currents of life, pain, love, and hope within ourselves. Silence is an opportunity in worship for the people to allow God to address them and let the Word evoke a response. Depending on the place of the silence, it may be an opportunity for confession, adoration, intercession, or the silent and ungovernable movement of God's Spirit.[29]

For many Christians, the Sunday liturgy will be the one place where worshipful silence can be a regular part of their lives. Thus it is extremely important that this element of worship, which cannot be legislated or written down in a manner to be followed, be sensitively created in worship. Certainly after the readings, in the confession, and during the intercessions, silence ought to be provided. People need time to discern how God is calling them, what is the connection between the world of Scripture and today's world, and how God's will is to be done on earth as in heaven. Silence is just as important during the liturgy of the Word as during communion. The form of the liturgy does well to allow explicitly for it.

Community Prayers. During the liturgy a variety of different prayers are uttered as expressions of the community's interconnection with God. After the initial Greeting, the presider and/or the entire community will often offer prayers of adoration (either a spoken prayer or a hymn such as the Gloria) or preparation (such as the Collect for Purity). A collect is prayed by the presider on behalf of the whole community, which either expresses our belief in some central aspect of God's reality or celebrates a dimension of the liturgical season.

Sometimes, near the beginning of the liturgy, a litany such as the Kyrie or a response to the Decalogue (a characteristically Calvinist expression) is uttered. Usually its purpose, if not a directly penitential one, is to remind us of God's call to be righteous and of our need to respond to that call, as well as our failure and need to be recalled to God's purpose for us. Often such litanies, like the liturgical use of the psalms, interweave strictly biblical language with extrabiblical words, using Scripture as a living confession of the present-day community.

The prayers of the people, in some form that allows for community participation, follow the Scripture readings. The community, having heard and reflected on God's word and intentions for our world, then exercises its priestly responsibility to pray for this world. The prayer is intended to be comprehensive and social, not dominated by individual concerns.

In the *Book of Common Prayer,* Cranmer titled it "For the Whole State of Christ's Church and for the World." Its provisions are universal in scope, to ensure that each gathering of God's people does exercise that priestly office for which it was baptized. In the prayers is also provision for each congregation and each member of it to prayer for particular local intentions. Contemporary Roman Catholic worship offers the chance for wide variety in the prayers and much local adaptation. Almost all contemporary liturgies encourage prayers that offer the congregation breadth of vision and specificity to a particular community.[30] Thus both catholic and very congregational dimensions of the church's worship can and ought to be expressed by the community.

Creed. The creed, used from the fifth century in the East, is a relative latecomer in the Western liturgy. It was not accepted in Rome until 1014.[31] Despite its late arrival, it took firm root in Sunday liturgies. In the sixteenth century, the Reformed tradition refused to require its use, but today most traditions use a creed or credal statement—if not the Nicene, then the Apostles' Creed or some more modern ones such as the UCC Statement of Faith. No matter what its form, the creed seems to respond to a basic need to utter a common profession of our faith in response to the Scripture read among us.

Thus the intention of the use of the creed in the liturgy is primarily doxological, as a hymn of praise of God, rather than as an intellectual test of faith.[32] How to make a common profession of faith, as distinguished from each individual's interpretation, is a concern that has always been a part of the church's worshiping life. Geoffrey Wainwright thoughtfully raises that question in his exploration of liturgical theology and suggests that we may best interpret the creeds in liturgy as poetry. That is not to claim that they have no "objective" content as a summary of the Christian faith. Rather they witness to the ancient faith and serve as a token of identity and continuity for the community.[33]

In the liturgy, as seems clear from the placement of the creed, its recitation or singing is intended to express a corporate pledge, in which all the members of the congregation affirm the faith of the communion of saints, rooted in the Scriptures and lived out over the centuries. The creed symbolizes our connection with the church's faith, and expresses our family identity.

The Kiss of Peace or "the Peace." In the early church the peace was a kiss and a greeting, offered to each other as an expression of the peace Christians extend to one another in the community because of the peace that they received from God. In the eucharistic liturgy it appears to have retained that form of a greeting and gesture. It concluded the synaxis after the dismissal of the catechumens, functioning as a sign of unity and communion among the faithful, thus forming an obvious bridge with the offertory.[34]

The kiss of peace has since migrated to various places in the liturgies of different churches. In the Roman Catholic Church, the kiss of peace has been restored to a community activity of mutual forgiveness and reconciliation and is offered directly before communion; in the Orthodox Churches it moved to a place immediately after the offertory begins. In Service of Word and Sacrament I of the United Church of Christ, it comes after the confession and assurance of pardon at the beginning of the service. In the Episcopal *Book of Common Prayer,* it is ordinarily in the same place as in the liturgy of the early church, performing the same role as the bridge between the Word and the Communion. (An optional rubric allows it also to be put at the beginning, similar to the Roman liturgy, or even at the time of the administration of the Sacrament.)

I think that the placement of the Peace in the liturgies of the early church is probably preferable, after the prayers of the people and the forgiveness of sins. In this context the Peace expresses our forgiveness and reconciliation in Jesus and our capacity and need to pray for one another and to seek a deepened community. The symbolism can be especially powerful if, in congregational worship, the Peace is an opportunity to express forgiveness of one another and welcome to the reconciled community gathering around the altar for the sacrificial meal of thanksgiving.

My purpose is not to drag the reader through extensive liturgical geography. I suspect that the variability of the place of the Peace and its reduction to a very disembodied gesture in many liturgies—for example, in the medieval West, kissing the cloth, called the *pax brede*—suggests a profound discomfort with the incarnational reality of the Peace. Contemporary uneasiness with the Peace, such as the arguments that it is distracting, undisciplined, too human-centered, alert us to a major difficulty we humans experience with the liturgy.

The kiss of peace, no matter how distant in manner, is face-to-face contact among human beings and sharing of a common gesture and word. Hymns, prayers, and listening to the Scripture and the Word proclaimed can be and usually are said or sung while the congregation and presider are facing each other or all are facing the altar. In that sense they are the congregation's actions in unison with God. But the peace carries the divine-human relation into the human realm.

As we exchange the kiss of peace with one another, the liturgy requires us to enact a new model of relations among us as a result of our relationship with God. Because God forgives us and makes us a new people in Jesus Christ, we are also now to forgive and to love one another, in word and in deed. I have been most powerfully reminded of the symbolic substance of the Peace, when in the midst of a parish conflict, some members refused to exchange the peace with others. At least they grasped the seriousness of the Peace. If full eucharistic discipline were in force, they would then absent themselves from Communion until they were able to say from their hearts as one sinful forgiven Christian to another, "God's peace be with you."

The peace thus can be volatile and subversive. Small wonder Christians often have not known what to with it in the eucharistic liturgy. But as an expression of our grateful response for the Gospel, our common life as forgiven sinners, and a pledge of mutual support, the Peace offers the most appropriate connection between the liturgy of the Word and Communion. The Peace allows all the people of God to express God's transformation of them through the Word they have received and responded to. The Peace pledges their common purpose truly to be God's people, joined in God's peace/shalom, and their readiness to gather around the eucharistic table, to be drawn together as one around one altar, sharing one eucharistic banquet, and being sent out in mission to God's world.

Having considered our liturgy of the Word, with our gathering as baptized Christians, our reading of Scripture, and our prayers, I want to focus with special concern in the next chapter on the sermon or homily. The sermon or homily is a part of the liturgy of the Word. Because it is the place in the liturgy in which the words of Scripture and today's world encounter each other most explicitly, it deserves special attention.

4.
Preaching
Incarnational Prayer

Preaching: What Do We Expect?

Raoul Rector had finally been invited to dinner by one of his parishioners. Raoul was a Floridian transplanted to New Hampshire and found New Englanders very distant and cool. Everyone seemed polite and correct, but they were never more than superficially friendly to him. At the door, after the ten a.m. Eucharist, everyone shook his hand and said, "Nice message, Father." After they all talked with each other at coffee hour, they waved or shook hands with him again, and left him to clean out the parish hall. He had been there for three months, and, aside from parishioners revealing the usual marital problems, psychological difficulties, and worries about next year's budget, he had no more notion of what made the congregation tick than he had on May 1, when he had first arrived at the rectory door.

Finally, the head of the ushers had invited him to lunch after the August 5 Sunday Eucharist and coffee hour. Raoul was delighted to receive the invitation. Fred had been the Chairperson of the Search Committee and always told him that he had given a good sermon and that the service was fine, because it was over in an hour. Having chased everyone out of the parish hall in record time, Raoul drove up to Fred's door with a spirit of eager anticipation.

Raoul could smell the barbecue sauce. Very quickly, however, his expectation of the barbecued pork changed to an expectation of barbecued priest. Fred, who had been as friendly and appreciative as any of his parishioners, stood straight in the doorway to the back yard and spoke soberly to Raoul. "Father, I invited you here because I needed to talk with you."

Raoul wished he had asked for a stronger drink and listened intently. "Father, it's about your sermons. You remember when we interviewed you how important we said good sermons were to us."

"Yes," Raoul replied, "I have tried to do my best. I spend ten hours a week studying and preparing. In each sermon I have done my best to connect the Scripture with real issues from the town and people's lives—the debate with the selectmen about whether nuclear waste would be stored here, the shock of discovering that the school principal was seducing third-graders for illicit photographs, the appalling level of adultery among the lay and clergy leadership in our churches. . . ."

"Stop!" cried Fred, brandishing the barbecue tongs. "That's the sort of thing we don't want you to talk about from the pulpit."

"But, you said you want me to preach about the Gospel and real life. . . ." spluttered Raoul.

"Hey, Father," Fred replied. "Life is tough. Get up at 6:30, fix breakfast, let the dog out in the yard, if you got little kids, get them up, dressed, fed, go to work, your boss hates your guts, you're afraid you'll lose your job, your mom's in a nursing home, your son's got AIDS, your blood pressure's up, et cetera! So I come to church, and what do I hear? How I'm supposed to change the world! Give me a break. Life is tough, and I just want you to make me feel better so I can get through it."

Sermon as Liturgical Prayer

A Practical Starting Point. As Fred the Head Usher and Raoul the Rector learned that Sunday afternoon, people's expectations about preaching are very strongly held, often quite different for different individuals, and usually unarticulated by anyone. I have had more than one conversation like that of Raoul and Fred. What can preacher and parishioner say to each other?

As we will explore in the next few pages, preaching is the most directly and overtly local liturgical prayer. In this chapter I want to sketch what I hope is a helpful theological perspective. But first, a few practical words cry out to be offered as an introduction to a broader theological approach.

In the local community, people come to worship for many reasons, some overtly religious and others much rooted in immediate personal problems and needs. The preacher's task is to connect as explicitly as possible people's immediate needs with the depth and breadth of Christian life and hope. The listener's role is to attend with critical openness to the preacher's utterance of the encounter between our lives here and now with the gracious and revealing words of Scripture. Both tasks require prayer, goodwill, and thoughtfulness.

People have any variety of motivations for attending church: lone-
liness and desire for social involvement, habit, death of a loved one,
problems in personal relations, desire to know more about God, love
of God, desire to please others, need for consistency amid change, anxiety because of life situations, and so forth. They are quite mixed,
some ongoing and others transitory, but they are present in virtually
every congregation, and often several are in each person.

All of us participate in the same community of faith, but quite frequently neither preacher nor congregation communicates clearly and
compassionately with each other. If preaching is to fulfill its role, it is
important for preacher and congregation to be clear about desires and
expectations for the sermon.[1] The preacher needs to know his or her
particular congregation, its motivations and expectations. The congregation's share in preaching begins with honest communication
with the preacher. Both preacher and congregation will want to find
nonthreatening, constructive, and truthful ways to articulate motives,
needs, and hopes in gathering for worship.

In preaching, the preacher will be most effective by first acknowledging that the congregation comes with many needs and hopes,
which need to be addressed in their diversity. Of course, the preacher
cannot address each individual, but explicit address needs to be made
of every kind of need from the desire to see God to the frustration of
the upkeep of a clean apartment or house for others. Of course they are
not all issues of the same magnitude, but they are part of people's lives
that, invisible as they may be, are brought into church as part of that
person.

Because we are all part of a worshiping community, not customers at
a supermarket, not all needs or desires are equal or of the same truth or
importance in the kingdom of God. It is not of equal importance that I
pray to experience and share with others the love of God, and that I
pray always to find a parking place. Liturgical preaching will strength-
en me in my desire to know and to give to others the love of God, and
it will lead me from my selfish but understandable desire to find a place
for my car into a Christian practice of life together in a community on
earth, where we share limited space and natural resources.

Christian transformation of life is the goal of preaching. Having
briefly identified some practical tactics, let us explore the deeper roots
of preaching and the transformation of our lives.

The Sermon's Theological Rooting. All preaching has its roots in worship.[2] Even "evangelistic preaching" is intrinsically linked to worship because of its preaching of the Gospel to convert people and draw them into the life of the worshiping community of God's people. Preaching is a part of the whole prayer that is the liturgy.

The sermon is the liturgical prayer that explicitly connects the Word of God proclaimed in the liturgy with our everyday lives. It thus grows from the integral reality of the worship of the people of God and is not an optional element. From the beginning it has been an essential part of the worship of the Christian community. The sermon is preached before God and the community, as an element of the dialogue between God and the community. In the sermon, as we remember our ancestors before God, our own lives are interwoven with God as we accept God's creative and sanctifying love into our own lives.

In the liturgy, human daily life and God's life are interconnected. Our very participation in the liturgy proclaims our radical intention to offer our whole lives and our world to God in order that we might receive into ourselves God's transforming grace. In each liturgical action, we hear the Scripture proclaimed to us and pray the prayers of Christians throughout the ages. We utter our struggles to connect ourselves with God's life. The prayers of the people and other specific references to particular situations explicitly connect the community's daily life with the universal scope of the liturgy. Usually these brief references are limited, individual, and almost formulaic—thanksgiving for q's new job, for the recovery of health of x, y, and z . . . .

From its beginnings, the sermon, however, was intended to be the moment of explicit, precise, and articulated connection of the community to the whole story of God's redemptive work in the world. Probably originating in the Jewish Diaspora, the sermon, in the sense of a discourse to the people about the Scripture, was preached to the people to instruct and edify them. By the end of the period of the Second Temple, the sermon in the synagogue or house of study was an integral part of Jewish practice. J. Hei describes the importance of the sermon to the continuance of Judaism:

> Through their reinterpretation of the Bible, their bold use of the biblical material to give expression to the burning issues of their own times, and the application of ancient traditions to new circum-

stances, the rabbis succeeded in keeping the Bible alive and meaningful for their own generations.[3]

From its very inception, preaching has founded itself on the assumption that Scripture and tradition are both time-bound, but also relevant to the lives of the present-day community. Some of the discourses of Philo show how he related and interpreted Scripture to the life of the Diaspora community in its adaptation of Hellenic culture to Jewish faith. His sermons offer written evidence that connecting Scripture and life is no simple task; rather, it demands a prayerful and pastoral application of rigorous thought.

The Christian community accepted also as its own the need to connect the Scripture and practices of its religious past with the present day life of the community. Jesus' preaching and teaching centered on the transformation of life necessary to live in the reign of God. God's kingdom was the topic of Jesus' prophetic preaching; Jesus proclaimed a realm into which the believers entered and the fulfillment of which they also anticipated at the end of time. Past, present, and future were connected in God's reign over all. His own words about the kingdom of God and its expectations adapt old teachings significantly to new circumstances. The Gospels relate Jesus' invitation to people to follow him into God's realm.[4]

Much of the debate about his authority revolved about debates over the kinds of adaptations of the Torah he made for first-century Palestinian life (see Matt. 5:17-48; 7:28-29). He interpreted the Sabbath commandment as "the Sabbath is made for humans, not humans for the Sabbath" (Mark 2:27). Jesus' preaching and teaching adapted his biblical tradition, sometimes radically transforming it. Such an approach depended on his God-derived authority and, equally important, on his conviction that he and his community were part of a continuing community of God's people, called to be faithful to God's will for humanity (see Mark 1:40-45; 2:23-28). His conflicts with the community around him grew from disputes about the right adaptation of Scripture to the present daily life of the community and about the very nature of the community (see Luke 10:25-42).

This vivid awareness of being part of an ongoing tradition that was also radically adaptable remained deeply rooted in the developing Christian community. After reminding its readers of the history of all the great people of faith throughout the centuries, the author of

Hebrews admonishes them to lay aside sin and remain faithful to the way of Jesus, "since we are surrounded by so great a cloud of witnesses" (Heb. 12:1-2). The author reminded these Christians that in many different ways and in varied times and places, people had expressed the same kind of faith in God and were citizens of one heavenly city (Heb. 11 and 12).

The preacher's task has always demanded both securely rooted communion with God and the possibility of sensitive and faithful adaptation of biblical tradition to present-day circumstances. God truly is revealed to the Christian community in the Scriptures. That divine self-revealing is understood by Christians to be normative, in the sense that God really is known to us. At the same time, we interpret this revelation of God through our reason and experience of God through out the ages. Our contemporary experience of God is formed and illumined through the Scriptures, and the Scriptures are constantly reinterpreted and seen anew in the light of the experiences of Christians throughout history.

Preaching and the Transformation of Life

When Justin Martyr describes the homily in the liturgy, he describes the president of the assembly: "When the preacher has finished, the president, in a discourse, admonishes and invites the people to practice these examples of virtue. . . ."[5] This first extrabiblical description of the sermon in the liturgy is described as connecting the tradition of the community with contemporary life. The rooting of Christian homiletics clearly is rooted in Jewish belief and practice and Jesus' own preaching of the reign of God.

All of us who preach and listen to sermons know how crucial is this interconnection between the God revealed in the Scriptures, the faith of the communion of saints, and our present-day searching and struggles. The sermon connects contemporary life with the living Christian story so that we in our world may willingly and knowingly be transformed by grace to be a part of God's new creation. Thus preaching grapples with the complexities of interpretation as different truth claims are expressed. The sermon also sets forth the challenges of Scripture as those address contemporary women and men in specific situations. Both preacher and congregation experience the formative power of Scripture in challenging and reshaping our lives.

In the sermon, the encounter between Scripture and our world is expressed in terms of daily life, rather than as an intellectual exercise or a set of moral imperatives. In describing the aspirations of African American preaching in the United States, Henry Mitchell identified one of its vital characteristics, which is at the root of all effective preaching. The preacher knows the people of the Bible so well that he or she can guide us into that world, be guide and interpreter, and help us see how the biblical world relates to our own.[6]

The preacher becomes so involved because the world of Scripture is as real to the preacher as Brooklyn, Fargo, or Sinking Springs. The preacher invites us to dirty our feet on the road to Jericho, where we hear the shrill cries of Bartimaeus, begging Jesus to let him see (Mark 10:46-52). But as we watch and listen, we realize that we are blind and need to see just as much as Bartimaeus. On Easter morning we watch in the chill of dawn as Mary Magdalene goes with the other women to Jesus' tomb. But when she meets Jesus in the garden, his words of commission to her confront the second-class treatment she has received in her world and often still does in our church (John 20:1-18). Our homiletic encounters with the biblical faith challenge and shape our belief and behavior, if we are willing to make the spiritual journey. A sermon that does not try for this goal may be eloquent entertainment or learned teaching, but it is not yet a sermon.

Certain specific elements are crucial to the sermon if it is to be an authentic and effective liturgical prayer for the transformation of our lives.

Sermon as the Expression of Christian Identity and Belief. A sermon is a cooperative work of preacher and congregation. Faith is the root, firmly connected to the life of God and God's people, adapting itself to varied times and situations. The growth of the people and of the preacher are interdependent; they are not two separate realities but elements of one plant, the driving energy of which is the life-force of faith. I do not believe that only the perfect or even the merely intensely virtuous are fit to be agents of God's redeeming love either in everyday life or in the formal ecclesiastical life of the church. Nor do I believe that only the virtuous or the learned ought to be members of the church. However, both virtue and learning are essential components of the exploration of Scripture in preaching that feeds our Christian lives.

Preaching is a dialogue in faith, not a spectator sport. The preacher is responsible for struggling to connect the two on the community's behalf. The congregation is expected to listen critically to the sermon and let it bring them into a closer encounter with God as God is revealed through the Scriptures prayed in the liturgy. The task for each sounds daunting; it is.[7]

In his description of African American preaching, Mitchell suggests that one of the great contributions it offers to all is its explicit recognition that the entire congregation is involved in preaching. Through body language, verbal responses, and occasional testimony, the congregation expresses its active involvement in the growth in faith which the preacher is articulating on behalf of all of them.[8] At its best, this congregational responsiveness guides and supports the preacher in articulating the community's shared belief and affirmation of appropriate response to God's call to us.

In the liturgy, the preacher is assigned the particular responsibility of exploring the complex landscapes of people's hearts and minds, as well as the whole social web of which they are a part. What is the economic state of the community, and how does it affect the people of the parish? For example, the parable of the poor widow (Luke 21:1-4) will be heard quite differently in prosperous times in a community where everyone has enough and a bit more, from how it is received in depressed economic times when people are unsure if they will be able to pay for housing, medical care, or food.

The preaching moment in liturgy reminds both congregation and preacher that Christians always live in two realms at the same time. We are citizens of this world, part of its life and work; we also belong to God's realm, God's world that is in this world and is yet to come in its completion.[9] The interrelationship of these two realms places the Christian in a constant creative tension. Over the course of centuries, the Christian response has been either to suggest that these two worlds have nothing to do with each other, or to insist that the goal of the Christian life is to pray and work for the transformation of this world into the realm of God's love and justice.

That disjunction between the present world in which we live and the world God intends us for is an easy one to make. Instead, the

Christian claims both/and rather than either/or. The world to come, the Christian asserts, is both an unmerited gift of God, and the transformation and perfection of the present world. The new creation is the re-creation, not the dissolution and replacement, of the present world. To flee from this world for another world not related to this one is to ignore the heart of the Gospel. Jesus prayed, "Your kingdom come. Your will be done on earth as it is in heaven."[10] The sermon helps us search out how we are endeavoring to bring God's realm to earth, as it is in heaven.

The preacher therefore seeks to involve the congregation in God's invitation to live life as Jesus in the Gospel calls us. The preacher cannot preach without some sense of the parishioners' relationship to this world and to God's word. Who are each of the parishioners? Quite happy and content with the faith of fathers and mothers? Seekers for new realms of spiritual insight? Unbelievers who want faith? Unbelievers supporting an institution of great social value? Social activists fed by a faith in God active among us? And so forth.

The congregation is a community that participates in the liturgy and in the sermon by active critical listening, prayerful reception, and discussion with the preacher outside the liturgy as the preacher prepares for the sermon. A hearer in the congregation who refuses to listen to the sermon, pays no attention, or seeks only something to criticize has yet to assent to being a member of the congregation. Such people are like family members alienated from all the other members. In addition to serious consideration of how to live his or her baptismal covenant commitment to community prayer, such a person would benefit from learning from other members of the congregation about how to participate actively and maturely in the liturgical prayer of the sermon.[11]

At the same time, the preacher is responsible to do everything possible not to alienate the members of the congregation. What scandal sermons offer if they are self-indulgent proclamations or ill-prepared meanderings. Only by respectfully attending to the thoughts and feelings of the congregation can the preacher offer the perspective of the Gospel for real people in their actual lives. Even if the preacher is impelled to condemn or question the faithfulness of the congregation, the sermon will be true and honest if it grows from the preacher's broad and deep encounter with the congregation in their world. The ideal of the Christian liturgy is for the preacher to listen to and understand the concerns of members of the congregation, so that she or he can struggle publicly with the Scripture on behalf of the entire community.

Sermon as an Expression of Personal Commitment. Personal commitment is a vital ingredient in both the hearing and preaching of sermons. Because a sermon is *liturgical prayer* that is a *testimony of belief,* both preacher and hearer who are living up to their parts in worship are participants in the life of the community, not detached observers. The preacher situates her- or himself within the congregation and integrates into the sermon, as much as humanly possible, its questions and concerns through the perspective of its liturgical leadership. The integrator is not, however, a computer or even a scriptwriter for a drama about a distant event. A living, breathing, believing, doubting human being preaches to a congregation composed of living, breathing, believing, doubting human beings.

A sermon will only be fully preached and prayed when the congregation honestly brings to the sermon its own beliefs and doubts, relationships, struggles, and all the circumstances of life. A preacher may be quite on the mark about the connection between Scripture and everyday life, but if the congregation wraps its life in protective coating to protect itself from the sermon, no living interaction can take place. A sermon is not passive entertainment but an invitation to the hearer to bring one's own life and the Gospel together so that one's life may be transformed. Such congregational participation requires a courage and commitment not often acknowledged by preacher or worshiper. The quality of our common prayer might be helped if we were more honest about the effort required for everyone's participation in the sermon.

One often unarticulated ingredient is required of the preacher. Vitally important to the preacher's life and work is the preacher's awareness about his or her own personal belief. When I began to teach preaching years ago, I would not have raised this issue so directly. In the course of teaching introductory preaching to seminarians, continuing education with clergy and laity, and my own pastoral work, I have become increasingly convinced that questions of belief and Christian identity are central to the personal and professional self-awareness of preachers today and to the honest participation of Christians in congregational worship.

We live in a society in transition. For each of us who preaches and each person who seriously listens to a sermon, that reality of change and uncertainty entails our willingness to risk honest and open admission of our own struggles with living our theology and ethics when our society does not agree on moral ground rules. The pressing reality of belonging to a multicultural society assures that no values are beyond question, and no religious or secular authority is accorded automatic acceptance or belief. Often, the unarticulated assumption is that only by destroying, ignoring, or denying present moral or social standards can a new culture emerge. The social structure that supports belief is often not present in the immediate community and rarely in the wider one.[12]

An effective sermon speaks the positive faith of the believing community—uttering for the gathered congregation the positive values of their faith for life in the world, even and perhaps especially in a time of societal conflict and uncertainty. Part of the intrinsic value of the sermon is its embodiment of the centrality and vitality of the interconnection between Scripture and life. A lively sermon, by its very occurrence, is an affirmation of belief in the ongoing involvement of God with the world.

Both preacher and congregation play their roles. In the act of preaching, the preacher is the designated representative of the ecclesial community, and the local worshiping congregation is the prism refracting the light between God and the world. A preacher who believes critically, reflectively, sometimes doubtfully and other times confidently, and always lovingly in the centrality of the message proclaimed will be a powerful testimony of the divine reality that the church has sought, served, and loved over the centuries. A preacher overcome by turmoil or cynical disbelief can provide the most powerful testimony possible against his or her own preaching. A congregation will find itself cultivating similar attitudes in its listening and practicing of the message proclaimed by the preacher.

The Sermon as the Hinge of the Liturgy. The sermon hinges together everyday life and the Scripture and tradition of the church. The sermon is also a hinge more directly in the liturgy. It connects the elements of the drama of the eucharistic liturgy itself.

How does the sermon in the liturgy connect everyday life with God and the whole life of God's people through time and space? The very position of the sermon in the liturgy suggests that it is the hinge connecting the liturgy of the Word—the reading of the Scriptures and prayers—with the eucharistic action. It is a hinge in two senses: First, chronologically, the sermon connects the two parts of the liturgy; second, the sermon makes explicit the faith in God revealed through the Scriptures that allows us to participate with integrity and holiness in the Eucharist.

Although there has been some debate about the unity of Word and Sacrament in the liturgy, most scholars would agree that the unity of the proclamation of the Word with the table liturgy is very early in the life of the church.[13] The sermon, which from the formative days of Christian liturgy followed the general model of the synagogue address, connects the hearing of the word and responsive prayers with the eucharistic Communion through what the Reformers called "explicit faith."[14] The sermon expresses the faith of the community, which hears the Word of God proclaimed and expresses its willingness to open itself to God's grace to transform it and to receive the life of God offered through the eucharistic sacrifice of Jesus.

The sermon utters the faith of the community in response to the Word proclaimed. What does this Word say to us in teaching and challenging us to transform our lives? How does the encounter of past generations with God help us in our own encounter with God? How does the Scripture invite us to transform ourselves and our world as the outcome of our meeting with God?

The sermon offers the breadth and width to explore how we might incarnate our faith today, in this time and space. In its entirety, the liturgy expresses God's saving encounter with the world and our response to God; the sermon focuses us in our time and space. This sermonic expression is essential in a liturgy that spans God's eternity and the spread of human history from creation to the eschaton. Without the sermon, the liturgy would be a general expression of faith, an anamnesis of God's saving work in the past, but the present would not be specified. The liturgy would remain abstract and generalized, without any recognition that what happened in the past is also present today.

In the context of the liturgy, the sermon testifies to God's eternal care for us. It also expresses the insistent call of God's living presence, that our world is made to be a part of God's realm on earth. The acceptance of God's reign is a decision to be made afresh, as we and our world constantly repent, return, and remake ourselves as God's own. Through the sermon each day's journey and each community's and individual's connection with God can be celebrated, and the joys and struggles explicitly interconnected with the story of the communion of saints.

If the faith of each community is not expressed and acted upon, the community's vision can dim, and its resolve can weaken. The sermon links us to the Gospel's invitation by exploring the vital question: How can we do it? How can we be faithful disciples here and now? How can we share in the doing of God's will on earth as in heaven? How can we here and now live God's promises given in ages past in the hope of a fulfillment to come?

A faith rooted in incarnation expects to have its faith continually made flesh and blood in concrete words and deeds. The sermon expresses the incarnation of God's love in our particular lives.[15] How is the creative, redeeming, and sanctifying love of God actualized in the life of Joan Jones on March 25, 1999, in Everett, Missouri, as she struggles with unemployment, personal depression, the possibility her children will have fewer economic opportunities than she had, and her hidden anger at God for letting all of this happen to her? The sermon is the liturgical opportunity for explicit utterance of faith, for the linking of the particular person and community with the whole sweep of God's involvement with the world. At the Holy Communion, we come to Christ's table, where we share in God's active transformation of our lives.

In the table liturgy, we offer the ordinary matter of the world and receive by tangible symbols the redemptive love of God transforming this ordinary life. The sermon articulates for us the reality of the many dimensions of the lives we live and their connection with the offering and receiving that we represent sacramentally in the communion. Through the Scripture, we hear God's word; at the altar we act out God's transforming love offered to us through Jesus' life, death, resurrection, and ascension. The sermon expresses how and why we share in the sacramental communion.

As we wrestle in the sermon with the why and how of our transformation in Christ, we prepare ourselves for our act of thanksgiving for who God is and what God is doing in us.[16] Preaching prepares us to stand at the altar, to offer and receive, to be empowered and commissioned, to be transformed and to share in God's transforming work. Through appeal to our minds and our hearts, the preacher utters words to evoke in us the desire and the will to join with the community of believers from all times and places who sing "holy, holy, holy" at the eternal liturgy.

Sermon as the Prayer for Transformation. The sermon is thus the most immediate and concrete expression of the particular worshiping community's participation in the transforming grace of the Eucharist. The sermon expresses the complex and varied nuances of the community's journey into the realm of God. In the sermon the most precise, trenchant, and direct exposure of the present world's reality can lead the congregation into an exploration of the process of conversation, and response to God's love. The preacher can explore with the community the process of transformation in grace evoked from the meeting of the needs and hopes of the people with the word of God proclaimed in the liturgy.

Our individualistic society pressures the preacher to offer a sermon that addresses each person's pains, problems, and desire for a one-on-one relationship with Jesus. There is a sense in which this desire is good and right. A sermon disconnected from a person's thoughts and feelings can never reach the one to whom it is addressed.

But if the aim of preaching is simply to cater to the individual's fancies, the preaching is distorted and misleading. Such preaching flees from history and seeks pure interiority. It assumes that all that matters is my feelings, my sense of connection with Jesus, and my safety in God. Such preaching directs itself to a realm that does not tackle the complexities of social life, and it assumes that the real person God cares about is the spiritual individual who is almost accidentally part of one time and place as distinguished from another. History is the dispensable trapping, and the "person" is what matters.

A Lutheran pastor of my acquaintance took a sabbatical to Germany and settled in a midsized city for a year. His German was fairly fluent, and he worked out an exchange with a German pastor who wanted to live in the United States for a year. Because he wanted to learn as much of the language and culture as possible, he decided not to prepare sermons, but simply to mine his colleague's library for German sermons. Late one Saturday evening, he grabbed a volume with a sermon for the appropriate Gospel. At the eleven o'clock service the next morning, he found himself praising the prayerful and studious habits developed by members of his congregation, as they prospered under the firm leadership of their beloved Chancellor Bismark.

As he heard himself, he vowed he would begin preaching his own sermons, even if wrestling with the German text was more work than he wanted to contend with. His conversion was not due simply to his embarrassment. As he looked about him, he realized that West Germany in the 1980s was vastly different from Bismark's Germany and that his congregants' lives grew in different soil these days. A responsible pastor, he learned, is one who takes account of the reality that although human nature is very much the same through the ages, historical context and social milieu are as important to the congregation as individual characteristics artificially placed in an atemporal setting.

The sermon leads us from the hearing of the Word and prayers to the altar not just as individuals who happen to live in a particular context, but as people intimately interconnected with their society. Humans are, as Aristotle noted, social animals. The sermon instructs and invites us as social creatures to participate in the growth and change the Eucharist offers us. It confronts head-on our impulses to flee into individualism or the anonymity of the crowd. The sermon addresses us as a part of the community, interconnected with the community, receiving and giving, affirming and critiquing.

Many Americans are children of a European Enlightenment that exalted the individual and rested its faith in the goodness of the individual when acting according to certain self-evident ethical principles. God guaranteed the moral order as creator of the natural order and judge after death of human behavior. The assumption of our forebears at the founding of the Republic was that this country would operate as the classical Greek republics had, with an ordered self-interest balancing the interests of others in a nation in which the basic freedoms allowed all a fundamental level of human dignity.

In fact, in the early American Republic, public life became dominated by competing economic interests. Power and influence accrued to the biggest force. The ideal of society's common good flew out the window, economic acquisitiveness become the common motivator, and the idea of a shared social idea shattered. Although from time to time secular theologians, such as Abraham Lincoln, affirmed the value of a united society, the internal fragmentation of society remains a primary issue for us even today.[17]

For preachers, a central concern is that in an increasingly fragmented society we seek a vision of the common good. We look for something that holds us together at the same time as we want our individuality respected. We are acutely aware of our common needs, our corporate sin as well as individual evils, and want some vision and a path to realizing our common good in this life as well as the next. A common good for the earthly city is a goal that increasing numbers of twentieth-century people share; as Christians we affirm a common good for our eternal future that shapes our notion of the world's common good.

The preacher's role is, with the active cooperation of the congregation, to connect our present situation with our past and to present before us the vision of the future that God wishes our present to become. The preacher interprets eschatology as it shapes our life in the present, as we pray and work for God's reign on earth. Our vision of the reign of God encompasses the rich expression of a varied community—the City of God, the wedding banquet of the Lamb, koinonia, the judgment with reward and punishment.

These images all express the dynamic of a community seeking its own transformation. Even though not everyone will agree on all particulars or all strategies and moral judgments, the Christian community seeks to apprehend and to utter the Gospel's call to us as we discern together what we humans need in order to become what God wants us to be and how best to move in that direction.[18]

Moving into God's Realm. "A thousand policemen directing the traffic/Cannot tell you why you come or where you go."[19] Eliot's words offer an important reminder that human beings cannot ultimately be moved by compulsion or external control. Only an internal vision and perception can effectively tell us both our origin and our destiny. The preacher articulates for the Christian assembly who we are and where we are going. In the case of our world's and our own ultimate destiny, no external policing is effective or justified; only our aspirations can direct us about how we can move toward our destiny, as well as where we are going.

Homiletic language about our destiny must of necessity be symbolic and imprecise, because that destiny is not yet realized; it is our future as well as present already in God. Discourse about how to move and grow toward that destiny can range from the more general to the very specific, because the issues of movement toward God's future for us can be related directly to the fabric of our world. The issues of social justice and community morality are an integral part of the worshiping community's growth toward God's realm on earth.

James Empereur and Christopher Kiesling have identified some of the key issues in liturgical preaching with its perspective on humanity's relationship to God's realm on earth. These issues remind us of relevant aspects of the Scriptures and their role in the liturgy:

> First, the Hebrew bible is an expression of the faith experience of an oppressed and powerless people. . . . While the kingdom of God is an eschatological reality, it is also a vision of this world being saved now. . . . Our worldly history is our salvation history. . . . Second, the bible as a religious reality is always a call to action . . . because the word [dabar] of God is. . . . Thirdly, the bible is essentially communitarian . . . .[20]

The preacher will find the tension between eschatology and present reality crucial to the exquisitely delicate connection that the sermon must make between present reality, the ideal future, and the way in which individuals and the community may best grow and move in that direction. The sermon thus never presents simple one-dimensional rules; it necessarily explores both motivations and varied actions as the people of God seek their freedom from all that hinders them from being what God created them to be and their freedom to become God's people living the fullness of life.

A variety of images in the Scripture point to the future reality toward which the people of God are living: the banquet of the lamb, the heavenly city, the new Jerusalem, the new creation, the heavenly sanctuary, the assembly of the saints, and so on. All of these images suggest the tension that the liturgy incarnates, that the fullness of life toward which we live is not yet here, and yet we already have glimpses, symbols, and anticipations.

We seek a transformed world in which God knows and loves us absolutely and at the same time in this love purifies and enlightens us. In this absolute love of God, we want to be drawn closer and closer to each other as we are at our best. We want to grow in that commingled experience of personal self-realization and complete interconnection with each other. We want this life to be an imperfect expression of the life into which we want to grow in God's eternity. The liturgy is a dramatic foretaste of what our whole lives anticipate; the sermon's work is to articulate that tension and at the same time to point out ways and directions in which we can hasten our transformation in that eschatological fullness.

Baptismal Covenant. In its baptismal liturgy, the church expresses the connection between our belief in God and our need to act in ways that bring us to the fullness of life for which God created us. A good preacher will find that good sermons about transformation will often make reference to Baptism. I remember one Sunday several years ago when I was baptizing the child of a clergy friend of mine. After my sermon, which was about Baptism and the Christian life, one of the older members of the congregation arose. "I've been going to church for 60 years," she said, "and I have never heard a sermon about Baptism."

Congregations today are, we hope, beneficiaries of our renewed theology of Baptism in the churches today, and often hear references to Baptism, the Baptismal Covenant, and our transformation in grace through God's saving love offered to us in Baptism. Sermonic references to Baptism and the Christian life explicitly connect the believer with the fundamental reality of his or her Christian life and offer an opportunity to remind congregations again of the intensely personal and utterly communitarian character of creation, sin, grace, and redemption.

For instance, in the United Methodist service of Holy Baptism, in the Renunciation of Sin and Profession of Faith, the question to the sponsors for children is "will you nurture *these children* [*persons*] in Christ's Holy Church, that by your teaching and example *they* may be guided to accept God's grace for *themselves,* to profess their faith openly, and to lead a Christian life?" The question to adults is even more explicit: "According to the grace given to you, will you remain *faithful members* of Christ's Holy Church and serve as Christ's *representatives* in the world?"

The Episcopal baptismal liturgy is even more explicit in its Covenant, which it directly connects with the affirmation of faith. As a continuous sequence, the three questions about the persons of the Trinity, which evoke the recitation of the Apostles' Creed, are followed by:

Celebrant:	Will you continue in the apostles teaching and fellow-ship, in the breaking of bread, and in the prayers?
People:	I will, with God's help.
Celebrant:	Will you preserve in resisting evil, and whenever you fall into sin, repent and return to the Lord?
People:	I will, with God's help.
Celebrant:	Will you proclaim by word and example the Good News of God in Christ?
People:	I will, with God's help.
Celebrant:	Will you seek and serve Christ in all persons, loving your neighbor as yourself?
People:	I will, with God's help.
Celebrant:	Will you strive for justice and peace among all people, and respect the dignity of every human being?
People:	I will, with God's help.

This development of the baptismal liturgy makes explicit what was assumed in previous liturgies, asserting it in a contemporary perspective.

Christian nurture for all ages provides sermons to insist that our Baptism is connected with what we believe God made the world to be and how we are going to act in order to move the world in that direction. As preaching more consistently offers such a perspective, Christians will grow up with the sense that in Baptism the Holy Spirit has made them God's people to do God's work, not offered them a celestial fire-insurance policy.

The churches have hundreds of years of individualistic teaching about Baptism to overcome. This conventional attitude toward Baptism removes from the believer any sense of belonging to the world as a Christian and having a role in the transforming of this world in the name of Christ. The good preacher will consistently and explicitly connect baptismal theology with Christian life in the world. Such preaching also will enrich the life of the community by explaining the intrinsic connection of Baptism, Eucharist, and Christian ethics.

Bread for the Journey

In ordinary travel, the journey and the destination are not usually directly related to each other. The traveler's questions about the process of travel are about cost, convenience, and pleasure. But the Christian life is different. Because the reign of God is both here and

not here and because our life and actions here and now are an anticipation of God's realm in its fullness, the way we move into God's
realm is utterly crucial. The journey and the destination are intimately interrelated. The preacher's role is to speak with the congregation
about how we are already anticipating God's realm and where we want
our actions to lead us.

This last statement may appear overly anthropomorphic. But it rests
on an assumption that God is truly and genuinely present among us in
Baptism, in the Eucharist, and in our preparation and preaching. Our
response to God is not passive, however, but invites us into a process of
cooperation with God's call to us. Thus how we respond and what we
do in praying and working for God's reign is of utmost importance.

The sermon is illuminator, motivator, and guide to God's people as
they seek to hear God's Word, interpret it for their particular situation,
live it in their individual and community lives, and let it guide them
into new and renewed ways of living the Christian life in a world that
may not share their beliefs. The sermon feeds us at each Eucharist as
we grow toward God's realm. Consistent and faithful preaching guides
us as individuals and as a community into God's realm.

One preacher has articulated the movement in preaching from considering the proclamation of the Good News of God's love to calling
for action in the world:

> But now it [the proclamation] must be made historical. Preaching
> can do that by calling people to live in communion with the Trini-
> tarian God, by urging the love of God in terms of solidarity with
> the poor, by offering the hope and motivation that we can live as
> brothers and sisters in Christ within a just society.[21]

Not everyone will agree about the ways the vision of God's realm is to
be made incarnate. The preacher will usually be wise not to be too specific, or at least to be humble in specificity. Directions, principles, and
critiques of government, society, and even the church in light of the
Gospel are very much in order in sermons; specific alliances with
political programs and telling people how to vote (ordinarily) are
quite out of order.

The preacher's complex and vital vocation is to speak to and for the
congregation about God's justice and love, truth and peace, so that we
can cooperate with God's call to us in our time and place. The sermon
is the designated liturgical moment to explore humbly but firmly

with people how, as the Spirit seems to be speaking to us, we can be and do God's Word of redeeming love. Oscar Romero wisely spoke of this delicate task of the preacher:

> People are free to choose the political system they want but not free to do whatever they feel like. They will have to be judged by God's justice in the political or social system they choose. God is the judge of all social systems. Neither the Gospel nor the Church can be monopolized by any political or social movement.[22]

5.
Eucharist
Communion and Community

In the first half of the twentieth century, two Christian poets wrestled with the relationship of God, community, and individual in Holy Communion. For each of the poets, a personal sense of isolation and search for communion and community run deep in their definition of being human before God. Their resolutions of this isolation through Communion are, however, quite distinct.

Charles Williams, an editor for Oxford Press, and himself a poet and novelist, wrote about Communion in a poem he titled from the liturgy, "At the 'Ye that do truly.'" He marks that moment as the time of division, contrasting with the common hearing of the Word, giving of alms, and profession of faith. The sincerity of penitence, or lack of it, divides us at the Communion time: "For penitence shall disallow/ Communion and propinquity." Penitence is the lonely barrier that will admit or deny the greater union in the communion with God in the Eucharist. But at the invitation to communion,

> Farewell! before this hour is done
> We shall have met or missed, my dear,
> In a remoter union,
> But now the solitudes are here.[1]

The second poem is by an earlier twentieth-century poet. Alice Meynall wrote of Communion in a different vein, instead focusing on *communion,* even when *separation* appears to characterize the liturgy.

> One of the crowd went up,
> And knelt before the Paten and the Cup,
> Received the Lord, returned in peace, and prayed
> Close to my side . . . .

She then prays to find Christ in this stranger close to her, because "this stranger who is thine—in all his strife" not only becomes the one in whom Christ lives, but is the one from whom Christ's grace may come to her. "Christ in his mystery! From that secret place/And from that separate dwelling, give me grace!"[2]

Both poems are rooted in a shared assumption: that we each are divided from the other by our individuality, our conscience, and varied other characteristics. But although the two poets are writing about the Christian's experience of Holy Communion, their approaches and their conclusions are significantly different. Williams finds that in Communion, even those of us most intimately related are deeply separated before God at the Communion by our consciences/moral selves and our individual relationships with God. Williams' theology in the poem takes as its root metaphor for Holy Communion Cranmer's late medieval version of the sinful and repentant Christian alone before God, the judge of our worthiness. Communion with God isolates us in any direct human sense, rendering us each alone before God, even after we have worshiped together in the earlier parts of the service. Our union in Communion is with God, not with each other.

Meynell articulates a different dynamic. For her, Communion ensures that Christ is known even in the stranger. She prays for the grace of the eucharistic Christ to reach out to her from the person next to her, whose only human relation to her is that of having shared the Communion and prayed near her. This grace of Christ can be the source of unity, speaking to her even from the mystery and "separate dwelling" of the other and dwelling in each, creating the communion between them.

What is the most profound problem that we seek to overcome in struggling to make our world better or even discovering in our lives deeper joy and hope? In the third or fourth century, someone probably would have responded that death and the fear of death was the great threat to human fulfillment. Luther in the sixteenth century would have surely replied that our guilt and sinfulness blocked the possibility of a relationship with God, which might give certain meaning to our lives.

Surely the dominant cry of our age would finally identify as our great issue our isolation as individuals and communities and our need to be connected with an ultimate reality in which we and our world have intellectual and emotional meaning.[3] For a Christian, our Communion in the Eucharist is that moment of faith when we find our deepest unity with God and each other.

The Sacrificial Meal: The Symbolic Action

The Holy Eucharist is a liturgy of Word and Sacrament, of hearing the Word of God and responding with prayer through words and gestures.

It is also, to borrow the venerable Augustinian phrase, the "visible word." Numerous Biblical images shape its identity: sacrifice (holocaust, communion, reparation), Passover, sacred meal, bread of life, messianic/eschatological meal, and others that spring from these (such as banquet of the Lamb).

The core metaphor for Communion is that of the sacrificial meal. Over the centuries, much ink has been spilled against the perceived exclusivity of the sacrificial tone of the Eucharist in the Roman Catholic Church during the late Middle Ages and post-Tridentine period. Today the most common description of the Eucharist in the ecumenical community is that it is certainly a meal, as the last few decades have explored in great depth. But it is a particular sort of meal, a sacrificial meal.[4]

Michael Downey, a contemporary theologian, has sketched this present-day understanding of sacrificial meal, noting the important work of the World Council of Churches' Faith and Order Commission and interconnecting the sacrificial meal image with the WCC categories used in *Baptism, Eucharist, and Ministry*.[5] All of these various categories can be linked together forcefully to interpret the Eucharist as the "celebration of the Easter community in the shadow of Calvary."[6]

The metaphor of the sacrificial meal has deep biblical roots, obvious dramatic dimensions, and all-encompassing implications for the whole of human life. Holy Communion is, based on this metaphor, a reenactment, a memorial. By memorial I mean an anamnesis. W. Jardine Grisbrooke notes quite rightly that the Greek word *anamnesis* is almost impossible to translate into English. When we speak of a memorial or remembrance, we mean that the person or event is "past and absent" and that we will remember what they have contributed to us. The Greek, however, "signifies exactly the opposite; it is an objective act, in and by which the person or event commemorated is brought into the realm of the here and now."[7]

In the prayer of the church, the sacrificial and redeeming crucifixion and resurrection of Jesus are remembered and enacted in prayer, and through God's faithful love, the gathered worshiping community is incorporated into the life of the crucified and risen Jesus. In this memorial of Jesus' sacrifice, the congregation acts to offer and receive the symbols of Jesus' life, death, and resurrection, and the life for humanity these symbols represent. All this action can be done only in and through the power of the Holy Spirit, who is the giver of life present and to come and who is sent by the Father through Jesus to transform the world.

The whole community gathers to pray, offer, and receive. The ritual actions of the presider at the gathering of the community are: present the community's offerings, bless and give thanks over the bread and wine, break and distribute the gifts so that all the baptized may receive, and (if the deacon does not) dismiss the people so that everyone may return to their mission and ministry in the world. The simple basic actions are those of a ritual sacrificial meal, in which the gifts offered are shared after being accepted and given back by the deity.

This deep mystic symbolism is ancient, even archaic. Nonetheless, its basic elements resonate with the deepest aspirations and needs of human beings. This sharing of the meal connects those who eat the meal with divine life and power and with others who also eat the meal. To eat the sacrificial meal affects the participants' behavior in the ordinary world.

As Gordon Lathrop notes, the Christian Eucharist requires a particular use of sacrifice as a metaphor, one that has been broken and restored to our use as the best way to express our redemption and reconciliation through the death and resurrection of Jesus. All we can offer is prayer, he asserts. We give ourselves as gifts, and in Baptism and Eucharist God accepts us through Jesus Christ in the Holy Spirit.[8] Lathrop is correct that "sacrifice" is a "broken" metaphor that God has given back to us to use for our sacrificial meal. Our actions and prayers do nothing; God's acceptance works our transformation. However, God gives us this particular symbol and metaphor not only to describe our worship, but also to shape our lives of response to God's gracious gift to us.

These simple actions of the sacrificial meal shape a drama that is symbolic and multidimensional, drawing together in itself the human connection with God and each other through the meal, the action of God giving and receiving, and the interconnection of the divine and the human. The sacrificial meal of the Eucharist is visible and invisible, matter charged with the life of God's Spirit and the relation of creation to God. This ancient form, acted at a particular moment in the present, also connects the present to the future. This connection is not simply a directing of people toward an undifferentiated future, but a meal in which those who eat and drink are transformed according to the image of God's coming world.

The Sacrificial Meal: What Is It?

John F. Deane, a contemporary poet, captures in the movement of the offertory at the Eucharist the meeting of divine and human in the making of the sacrificial meal. We offer the bread, which becomes the symbol of human agriculture, trade, and transport linking us with many lands. We offer the wine, which symbolizes the pain of human labor, exploitation, and unrest even in far-off lands. Bread and wine are offered to Christ, and in return we pray:

> Then give into our hands
>   your flesh
>   to melt and merge with the soil and the stones.
> And give into our hearts
>   your blood
>   to seep through the sweat when the world groans;
> that our earth may grow through its brightest blackest parts
> a sight well pleasing to the Lord of lands.[9]

Deane's poem expresses graphically the simple action and the complexity of the sacrificial meal we call the "Eucharist." It weaves together all the elements of ritual reenactment, God's healing and redeeming love, human offering and receptiveness, and the transformation of the world through this creative love.

It is difficult to speak of sacrifice in our North American world today. All too often "sacrifice" has been part of religious language to pacify the poor and powerless, both as individuals and as groups. Dominant persons and classes have heard and used the same words about sacrifice but have seldom practiced it. Even when they did sacrifice their own goods, they seldom moved beyond the realm of the highly personal and individualistic. If this is sacrifice, no wonder people reject it. The misuse of the ideal of sacrifice has been a sad perversion of the core of our eucharistic faith. Moving poetry, the witness of other religious faiths, and a return to our own authentic biblical roots may give us a clearer vision of what the biblical notion of sacrifice is.

A participant in the Lakota Sun Dance spoke vividly of the Sun Dance and the dancers who fast and dance for three days, attached with hooks to the great pole that reaches up from the earth toward the sun. She said simply: "Our Indian way of life is a hard way. But it makes us strong." She held up a notion of sacrifice that is costly and empowering, not demeaning or impoverishing. She also identified another aspect of sacrifice, that sacrifice connects one firmly with the divine and with the human community. These elements are all aspects of the biblical understanding of sacrifice, which certainly is in tension with our own culture. It moved me deeply to hear someone from another religious tradition utter the profound value of sacrifice for the human heart, and I asked myself about the cost and empowerment of sacrifice in the Christian tradition.

Biblical Perspective. One never finds a justification of sacrifice in the Bible; it is simply assumed to be a part of life as essential as breathing. Because God is the sovereign and creator of the world and ruler of the people, sacrifice is rightly given to God. That reality is an obvious and crucial fact of life. The Hebrew Bible asks only about what sort of sacrifices are to be made and about ritual and ethical connections between the sacrifices and the worshipers' life.

The whole ancient Middle East assumed that sacrifices to the deities are essential to the order of the world. In the *Epic of Gilgamesh*, when Utna-pishtim (a prototype for Noah in Genesis) walks onto the dry land, he immediately builds an altar for blood sacrifice to the gods and goddesses. We read that they draw around the altar like flies to the carcass. Utna-pishtim is spared from the destruction wrought on humans by the flood because he will obey and offer sacrifices; the deities require his gifts. His sacrifices are gifts offered to the deities to benefit them; humans prosper because the deities favor them for their obedience and gifts. Sacrifice is food that nourishes the gods and goddesses.

The Hebrew Bible interprets sacrifice quite differently. The Israelites believe, as do the peoples around them, that human beings must offer sacrifice to the divine reality. But as the people's understanding of God becomes clearer, especially in connection with God as universal creator, they realize that God does not need their sacrifices. Psalm 50, after praising God as the righteous judge, lets God say to the people that the One who is the creator of all does not need bulls or goats to eat or drink their blood, the life force.

Instead, the people are warned: "Offer to God a sacrifice of thanksgiving, and pay your vows to the Most High" (Ps. 50:14). The text reflects the tension in the religion of Israel, which is not focused on whether or not to offer sacrifice but on what sort of sacrifice must be offered to God and to what end. The Hebrew Bible describes a quite elaborate system of cultic worship as the focus for the people's covenant connection with God. The function of sacrifice is not to supply God with something lacking or needed, but to establish and strengthen the people's connection with God.

Three major forms of sacrifice, depending on circumstances, are to be offered to God: communion, gift, and sin offerings. The communion sacrifice described in Leviticus 7 is an important root of the Christian understanding of the Eucharist as sacrificial meal. In the thanksgiving offering, both grain and animal offerings are presented to God. Part is burnt on God's altar, part belongs to the priests, and part is given to the worshipers, who eat it on the first and second days of the sacrifice. Then the holy food is destroyed. The ritual surrounding the consumption of the offerings by the worshipers emphasizes the sacred bond of communion with God created by eating the food offered to God.

Whatever the type of sacrifice, in each the worshiper must follow an elaborate observance for ritual purity. In part at least, this is because the worshiper ritually identifies with the sacrifice, and thus through the sacrifice is accepted by God (Lev. 1:4; 3:2). This aspect of communion between God and the worshiper is at the heart of all sacrifice (Deut. 12:7; Exod. 18:12). The elaborate codes in Exodus, Leviticus, and Numbers all govern this complex relationship.

Although not precisely the same sacrificial meal as described in Leviticus, the Passover ritual described in Exodus 12–13 has, as Stephenson notes, elements of the sacrificial meal. The lamb's blood on the lintels alleviates God's wrath, but the meal itself is a commemoration of God's mighty acts. The Passover meal, although probably not the liturgical model for the Eucharist, certainly suffuses the spirit of the Christian Eucharist as a meal in which the people's deliverance, redemption, and communion with God are primary components.[10]

The Atonement Day sacrifice, which is prescribed in Leviticus 16 and 23 and looms large in Christian theology, is not a sacrificial meal. However, the identification between the priest, acting on behalf of the people, and the sacrificial victims, is a fundamental element of God's acceptance of the offering. The victims' sacrifice is essential to the ritual of God's forgiveness of the people's sins. Without God's acceptance of the people's offering and forgiveness of the people, communion with God would be impossible.

The worshipers' self-identification with the offerings made to God is an essential element of worship (Lev. 1:4; 3:2). The victim represents the worshiper in being offered to God. The ritual laws applicable to worshiper, victim, and priest all serve to emphasize the connection the sacrifice makes between the worshiper and God. Consequently, because the worshiper through the sacrificial ritual has been offered to God, the worshiper's moral behavior and purity of heart are considered intrinsic to God's acceptance of Israel's sacrifice (see Mal. 3).

Morality as an integral element of the sacrificial cult became increasingly emphasized in the development of the religion of Israel. Worship and behavior in daily life were understood as necessarily connected. Thus, the cultic sacrifices are expected to be accompanied by the acts of justice that the Law also demands (Isa. 1:11-17; Amos 5:21-22). The burden of the prophets' preaching is not to attack the cultic system as such, but to insist on obedience to all of God's Covenant Law.

God's Covenant with the people, if truly followed, unites external worship with internal purity and good actions toward others. Without justice, the sacrifices are in vain because there is no true communion between God and neighbor with the worshiper. Worship and obedience to all the commandments are intrinsic elements of human life lived according to the Torah.

The famous sermon of Jeremiah (ch. 7) outside the Temple is a good exemplar of this prophetic approach to sacrifice. Jeremiah excoriates the people for not living according to God's command even though God led them from Egypt and slavery into freedom. God spoke not about sacrifice, but about obedience. The abomination is not that the people sacrifice to God, but that they do not do the works of justice, and thus they make their sacrifices a mockery to God. Their disobedience is as offensive to God as the idolatry of those who "make cakes for the queen of heaven."

Within this context, one should note that right/just relations between the members of God's people are integral to the sacrifice and communion with God. Moral and ethical treatment of each other is a necessary dimension of communion with God. In the prophets, moral treatment of each other is understood as a prerequisite of communion with God through ritual sacrifices. God hates and rejects "new moons and appointed festivals" unless the people will "seek justice, rescue the oppressed, defend the orphan, plead for the widow" (Isa. 1:14-17).

New Testament. During his lifetime, Jesus appears to have observed the cultic worship of Israel but challenged its ritual purity laws. From the perspective of the prophetic tradition, he focused on the necessity of internal purity, prayer, and the doing of good for one another as essential to the Law and Israel's worship (see Mark 11–12).[11] After Jesus' death and resurrection, his followers developed their understanding that it was through Jesus that we have access to God and by following Jesus' teachings that we know how to live.

The Christian community soon developed the understanding that Jesus' death is the unique and definitive sacrifice to God; no more is needed (Heb. 9:11-12, 24-25). Jesus' sacrifice is unique because through it humanity is transformed. The separation of human life from God's life is healed and reconciled through Jesus' sacrifice and humanity's acceptance into God. The believers' life is bound together with Christ, and therefore the Christian way of life becomes a part of the baptized person's acceptable sacrifice to God, in and through Jesus.

The worship Christians offer through Baptism and Eucharist expresses this interconnection among Jesus, Christian believers, and God. Baptism is like the new Exodus, bringing freedom from sin and death to the baptized (1 Cor. 10:1-4). Like Noah's ark, it protects the baptized, the new Israel, through a "pure conscience" given through the risen and ascended Jesus (1 Peter 3:21). Paul elaborated a complex theology of Baptism in which the believer dies and rises in Christ and thus becomes eternally connected with Christ and Christ's life (Rom. 6). In Johannine theology, Baptism is compared to a new birth (John 3:4-5).

All of those themes describe how the believer becomes one of God's people, joined as one with Christ who, as the perfect sacrifice, has died, is utterly accepted by God, and rises from the dead, empowered to transform all who believe in him. Unity with Jesus comes through life in the Holy Spirit, not the spirit of this world. Through Baptism, the believer becomes one with other believers, part of one body, the body of Christ (Phil. 4:1-6). An essential part of the baptismal theology is the conviction that the baptized Christian is commissioned to continue the redemptive work of Jesus through transforming the world in Christ's name by spiritual, moral behavior (Rom. 8:1-17; 13:8-14).

Thus the language and assumptions of the Christian sacrifice are substantially different from the Hebrew Bible's approach. In the Jewish sacrificial system, the various sacrifices express an interior attitude, such as repentance or gratitude, or are obedient fulfillments of the ritual law. In the New Testament's interpretation of Jesus' death, including the use of the language and imagery of sacrifice to describe it, the meaning of sacrifice shifts to an event transformative of the Christian. This transformative event includes all who share in the cultic acts that, in the church, connect the believer with Jesus.

Because the sacrifice of Jesus is transformative, Eucharist is the food for the journey, the sacrificial communion meal in which Jesus is understood in the Christian community as both remembered and present as the food of eternal life (1 Cor. 11-12; John 6). Whether regarded as the Passover meal or the religious fellowship meal, the Eucharist quickly took on the character of a sacrificial meal, ritually influenced and shaped by synagogue worship. In the Eucharist, Jesus is the Paschal Lamb, and the gathered community shares in communion with God through eating the Lord's day feast (1 Cor. 5:7-8).[12]

The institution narratives in the Gospels and in 1 Corinthians echo the language of sacrificial cult: "my body given . . . my blood poured out . . ." (Matt. 26:26-29; Mark 14:22-25; Luke 22:14-22; 1 Cor. 11:23-26). The body and blood of Jesus are sacrificed to God and are to be shared by the disciples so that they can share life with Jesus in God's realm.

Thus the sacrificial language points to communion with God, but also with Christ and with each other. "And Christ died for all, so that those who live might live no longer for themselves, but for the one who died and was raised for them" (2 Cor. 5:15). Because the believer is part of the body of Christ, the baptized Christian will behave according to Jesus' ethical demands and expectations in the whole of life with regard to all people (Phil. 2:1-11). Therefore, communion with God through Baptism and the Eucharist has specific ethical consequences for the whole of Christian life.

Through the sacrifice of Jesus and our sharing in it through Baptism and Eucharist in the Church, we belong to God just as Jesus does. Ritual and ethical life are integrally connected because of the communion between Jesus and the believer. Thus the baptized person can be spoken of as a sacrifice or sacrificing in Jesus, and the actions of one's life as acceptable offering in and through Jesus (Rom. 12:1; Phil. 2:17; Heb. 13:15-16). The connection between everyday actions as acceptable offerings and the self-offering of Jesus provides the rooting and grounding for Christian morality and its involvement with each aspect of daily life.

Thus everything the baptized person does is intended to be an expression of God's justice and compassionate love, because the believer is accepted totally and completely by God, just as Jesus was. For the early church, Paul's cry, "Now no longer do I live, but God lives in me" (Gal. 2:20), is not an emotive exclamation but a vivid expression of fundamental belief. The consequences of such life in God is that all of one's thoughts and deeds are to be expressions of God's life, just as Jesus was and is such an expression.

Luke's Gospel and Acts of the Apostles continue this line of thought—to set up a sort of applied Christian socialism as the ideal for the Christian life (Luke 6:20-26; Acts 2:43-47; 4:32-34). Belonging to God means in practice that everything one is and has must be used for God's purposes. One's self in communion with God through Jesus, with one's worship and one's goods, is sacrifice to God and no longer one's own. That is because through Baptism and Eucharist, one is no longer simply one's own person, but God's in Christ. Thus every action from the most rarefied spiritual ecstasy to washing dishes to giving money are all essential parts of the life of the believer, who is God's and who thus lives God's life in and to the world.

Historical Development. A historical perspective suggests that even though the theology of the Eucharist might be expressed differently in various places and times, there is always a clear connection between Eucharist and daily behavior. The early church understood the Eucharist as the *via tecum* (bread for life on the journey) for the Christian life, food for the journey, the sacrificial meal of the self-revealing and giving God, and a foretaste of the heavenly banquet of the saints delivered from death and at one with God and the Lamb of God.

Already in Paul's admonitions to the Corinthians (1 Cor. 11–13), we find expression of the direct relationship perceived between sharing in the eucharistic banquet and behavior in ordinary life. The early church continued this emphasis, not hesitating to insist on the economic as well as the spiritual obligation to each other of Christians fed at the same table. Clement of Rome reproached those who came to the eucharistic sacrifice without their "gifts" for the poor as well. Much emphasis was placed on the necessity and justice of giving to the poor.

Many of the church leaders, such as Augustine and John Chrysostom, fought against the notion of absolute property rights. They argued that all property belonged to God and to God's people. Christians could not own property; they could only hold it in trust for the community.[13] Those who prayed these early liturgies understood the Eucharist as a sacrifice in which we are not passive observers. In and through Christ, we offer ourselves and our goods to God. The offertory, which includes bringing both the bread and wine for the eucharistic meal and alms for the poor and the support of the church, was understood as essential to the Eucharist. The way in which this offering was ritualized might differ, but all expressions were undergirded by the holistic vision of the offering of the "stuff" of everyday life for God's restoration of the whole world.[14]

The gap between participation in the Eucharist and its integral relation to everyday life grew. In part this was because the liturgical language changed from the vernacular to Latin and in part because the congregation was increasingly excluded from active participation. The Mass was a drama that showed the congregation the passion and death of Jesus and pointed to the eschatological fulfillment of the world in heaven. The believer watched but ordinarily was passive except for silent prayer and meditation. Some of the ritual of money or in-kind offerings was retained at the offertory or taken before or after the Mass, but the theological roots and connection between participation in the Eucharist and daily life were neglected. Attendance at the Mass was regarded as an important moral and religious instruction, from which the believer was to learn and be edified. Although the ideal was a laicized version of monastic meditation, for the uneducated, elements of magic were part of their participation in the Eucharist. It became a time for "seeing Jesus" in the host and gaining safety and protection from this act. The Mass became for many both a focus for prayer and also a magical charm.[15]

The Reformers struggled through their liturgical changes to link together again more clearly and closely the daily life of the believer and the sacrificial meal of the Eucharist. Protestant and Anglican worship in various ways endeavored to express the involvement and participation of all the baptized in the Eucharist and to shape the rituals to stress involvement of all; Roman Catholic piety found ways to include the people in the liturgy, but not as active participants and actors in the eucharistic offering of life and gifts.[16]

Today's Reshaping of the Liturgy. The nineteenth- and twentieth-century Liturgical Revival in Protestant and Catholic circles has reshaped our understandings and our liturgies. The revival has moved Catholic, Protestant, and Anglican churches through a shift from individual devotion to active participation of the whole gathered community, use of a fuller eucharistic prayer, making an explicit connection between the Eucharist and daily life, and increased sensitivity to local context.[17] As Western society, and thus global culture as influenced and shaped by Europe and North America, views the holy and the everyday as necessarily and perhaps intrinsically separated, their reintegration becomes increasingly vital to the life of the Christian community.

Members of the Christian community individually and corporately want to know or be reassured that there is a connection between the world of God and church and the everyday world of work. When society doesn't offer such reassurance, the liturgy's role is even more crucial. The sociologist Robert Bocock notes that "the new liturgies rest on the idea of bringing the common and the holy together."[18] Because the great spiritual issue of our time is the struggle to reconnect our lives and our world with Ultimate Reality, the liturgy becomes the locus where that effort is explicitly undertaken, the moment of encounter of our experienced world with the divine.[19]

How is this done? Bocock cites Durkheim's description of sacrifice, with its two essential elements of the act of communion and the act of oblation. The Holy Communion includes the offering by the congregation of material of its daily life, symbolized by money, as well as the food that will be consumed during the sacred meal. The second element is the eating of a sacred food that is both communion with the

Holy and sharing in a human offering (the food brought at the offertory and the offered life of Jesus, who is both human and divine).[20]

This classic vision of the Eucharist serves to respond to the contemporary need for reintegration of life. It is part of a basic act of personal and corporate interconnection of humanity and the divine in the real world in which people live. With its integrative capacity, it is a ritual action that has profound moral power. Such integration empowers the participants to live into God's reign of justice and peace.

The transforming power of the Eucharist is exercised, according to this sociological analysis, through the symbolism and emotional structure through which the ritual affects the participants. The liturgy of the Word, with its prayers, Scripture readings and preaching, is intended to offer spiritual and moral guidance about everyday life. As Bocock notes, the ritual does not presume that all of the worshipers "live up to their ideals and moral values, but that they are guided by them." He writes that in the communion, through the ritual offering, consecrating, and sharing of the bread and wine, "the people come into direct contact with the sacred.[21] In this action the possibilities are opened for transformation of the worshiper, and through this transformation, the reintegration of the sacred with the world.

Eucharistic Prayer: The Dramatic Elements

The drama of the transforming sacrificial meal of the Eucharist is deeply rooted in the worship of the church. In his classic work, *The Shape of the Liturgy,* Gregory Dix identified four invariable actions that explicitly characterized all ancient eucharistic rites:

> (1) The offertory; bread and wine are "taken" and placed on the table together. (2) The prayer; the president gives thanks to God over bread and wine together. (3) The fraction; the bread is broken. (4) The communion; the bread and wine are distributed together.[22]

After the prayers of gathering, readings from Scripture, sermon, prayers and exchange of the peace, the eucharistic action (synaxis) begins.

The way in which the eucharistic action is enacted is crucial to its symbolic power and function. Davies notes that the Eucharist is not an interruption, no matter how holy, to everyday life, but is "co-extensive with the whole of our existence."[23] Because that is so, the way in which the eucharistic ritual expresses the whole of human experience is particularly important.

For instance, if at the end of the "Holy, holy . . ." all of the members of the congregation falls to their knees in individual pews and never lift their heads until Communion, the ritual clearly expresses a religious culture of isolation, hiding from God and from the world, and dissociation of each worshiper from the other. If everyone sits in the pews and listens to someone read the story about the Last Supper and then bread and grape juice are passed to people in the pews by the deacons, intellectual remembrance, physical and emotional passivity, and individual isolation become the hallmarks of the Communion service.

Depending on the architecture and the mobility of the furniture, gathering the congregation around the altar/table is certainly the most desirable practice, because it dramatizes the community joined actively as one. The physical character of the people standing (or sitting on benches arranged close to the altar for those unable to stand), singing, and speaking their part in the dialogue is fundamental in expressing the action of the community in the Eucharist. The community presents its offering and gathers with the priest or minister the church has designated to exercise the eucharistic leadership in the community.

All gather together around the altar, with the bread and wine, and all are transformed in Christ and pray for the transformation of the entire world. All take communion as the pledge, sign, and seal of their identity as disciples in mission to the world. All depart from that altar or perhaps from the pews where they have returned to gather their belongings. Perhaps they will go into the coffee hour to continue their community, or perhaps they will go directly out into the world. However they go, strengthened by words and music, their bodies will have expressed the power and purpose of the great ritual in which infinite love and redemptive suffering are united for the world.

Each community, with its individual church building, insights, and abilities in music and the other arts, will find various ways to express the unity of the community, its renewal in the sacrificial death and resurrection of Jesus, and God's infinite love for the world. The critical necessity for authentic worship in each community is to express the internal as well as the external dynamic of the eucharistic meal.

"Authenticity," of course, does not mean 100 percent agreement of every member of the community, but a specific shape to the Eucharist that enables members of the community to express their faith and to be formed and educated by the Eucharist. The community Eucharist thus becomes a familiar sustaining reminder of God's love and the personal as well as cosmic significance of suffering; it also pushes, shoves, and reshapes us as believers interconnecting the Holy and the worldly through the best incarnation of worship that the community can offer at any given time.

The Movement of the Liturgy. John A. T. Robinson offers a very strong observation about the power of the communion liturgy.

> When we come to Communion it is to the very drama of our redemption that we come, in the literal and original sense of that word drama, 'the thing done.' We come not simply to a miming of it, as to a passion play, but to the thing done itself, or rather to the doing of it. For we come here to the Cross, to Lord's death. And here too we come to the Consummation: we enter that new world to which already by Baptism we belong. For at this point both past and present converge upon the present.[24]

Thus, as Robinson reminds us, the communion is both a sacramental action in which we enter into the eternal time in which we are incorporated into the passion, death, and resurrection of Jesus, and also our contact with the new Creation into which God is making us and this world. Thus the intrinsic necessity of the liturgical action of the communion expresses both what is happening in us here and now, and also our hope for the new world which God is making in and through us.

Offertory. After the greeting of peace, which those forgiven and reconciled in Christ offer one another, the offertory begins. Different ways of ritualizing the offertory have developed over time in the liturgy. Sometimes the ritual has been quite elaborate and included processions with bread and wine, money, and other rich gifts. It has been truncated, as in the medieval Latin rite, with the bread and wine kept on the credence table to be hurried to the altar at the time of the preparation of the chalice and paten. Sometimes, in the Greek liturgy, the ritual has separated the ritualized preparation and offering of bread and wine from those of other gifts of the people.

The central reality of the offertory is, however, simple and constant: the ordinary material of life—bread and wine as the chief symbols—

are offered by the congregation to be transformed through the power of the Holy Spirit into the redemptive mystery that is new life for the world. The bread and wine are the matter of everyday life; these two forms of food and drink symbolize both the food and drink that sustain us and also the labor of body and mind and order in society that are necessary to produce them. Responding to God's invitation, humans dare to offer those gifts. Historically, all the people contribute to the gift offered, and designated members, usually deacons, place it, or representative gifts, on the altar.

Since at least the second century, money and other offerings have also been received as a part of the offertory action at the Eucharist.[25] The intrinsic obligation of the Christian community to care for its members was from biblical times understood as an essential part of Christian life and worship. Because the Eucharist is an agent of transforming society, it is crucial that the people offer in a sacred action the money that is the product and sign of a social and economic order being transformed in Christ.

The return and ritualization of the collection of the people's gifts into the Eucharist was an important contribution of the post-Reformation church, especially Anglicanism. This reform of the offertory ritual integrated the offering of money and of bread and wine as part of one action, in which both bread and wine and money are placed on the altar as the congregation's offering and openness to God's transforming grace in the whole world.[26] As Iddings Bell noted, the Offertory thus combines our human offering of our work and our common life to God.[27]

The Prayers of Blessing. When the bread, wine, and other offerings have been gathered and prepared for the prayers of blessing, the community joins around the altar/table with its liturgical leader to offer its prayer to God. Although over the course of two thousand years, a wide variety of prayers and action have been used, the contemporary consensus tries to follow the practice of the early church, as best can be recovered and adapted. The World Council of Churches' *Baptism, Eucharist, and Ministry* identifies the elements of the eucharistic prayer after the offertory that are generally received as constitutive by Christians today:

- thanksgiving to the Father for the marvels of creation, redemption, and sanctification . . .

- the words of Christ's institution of the sacrament according to the New Testament tradition;
- the anamnesis or memorial of the great acts of redemption, passion, death, resurrection, ascension, and Pentecost, which brought the Church into being;
- the invocation of the Holy Spirit (epiclesis) on the community, and the elements of bread and wine . . .
- consecration of the faithful to God;
- reference to the communion of saints;
- prayer for the return of the Lord and the definitive manifestation of his Kingdom;
- the Amen of the whole community;
- the Lord's prayer;
- sign of reconciliation and peace;
- the breaking of the bread;
- eating and drinking in communion with Christ and with each member of the Church;
- final act of praise;
- blessing and sending.[28]

The sweep of the eucharistic action makes clear that in the eternal reality of the Cross and Resurrection, we offer and receive back from God through Christ our "interests and activities redeemed and transformed . . . ."[29] Our lives and gifts are accepted into the gift and offering of Jesus—his sacrifice and communion with God, which transform us and our world. The various prayers put our particular eucharistic celebrations in the context of the eternal redeeming love of God. Our human story and offering is incorporated into God's great action of creation, redemption, and sanctifying us and all creation.

The eucharistic prayers not only situate us in the great cosmic drama of creation, incarnation, cross and resurrection, and the coming of the Spirit, but also point us to the fullness of time, when God's transformation of the world will be completed in this present order. Calvin understood the Eucharist as the anticipation of the heavenly banquet through our becoming present in heaven at the Eucharist; in Orthodox theology, the liturgy brings heaven to earth. Contemporary eucharistic prayers struggle to express the eschatological dimensions of the liturgy and the life of the church in the world.[30]

In all contemporary liturgies, a part of the communion prayers is always the recital of the mighty acts of God and an expression of longing for God's re-creation of this world. The Eucharist is not a prayer for our deliverance from this world, but a prayer for transformation and healing of this world in which we live. For instance, Prayer B of the American *Book of Common Prayer* asks God, "In the fullness of time, put all things in subjection under your Christ . . . ." Most liturgies still formulate this connection with Christ and the recreation of the world in terms of service (for example, United Methodist Service of Word and Table I, United Church of Christ Service of Word and Sacrament II). The Eucharist as the vision and anticipation of this whole world transformed in Christ is still only weakly articulated in the eucharistic prayers. The whole universe is explicitly included in praise of God in such prayers as the "Holy, Holy, Holy" used in virtually all eucharistic liturgies.

Prayers C and D of Rite II in the Episcopal *Book of Common Prayer* also use cosmic perspectives: C a contemporary expression and D an adaptation of the Prayer of St. Basil. In the same prayer book, the Order for Celebrating the Holy Eucharist (which cannot be used at the main Eucharist on a Sunday) allows the celebrant to adapt the proper preface to the particular occasion being celebrated, within the context of God's saving work. In the new Roman Rite, the proper prefaces connect the seasonal celebration of God's gracious activity among us with the worship of God by the congregation and the eternal worship of God in heaven.

Geoffrey Wainwright describes the Eucharist as a taste of the kingdom to come and a sign of the kingdom that is coming among us.[31] The Eucharist thus already is a sign of what the reign of God will be, as well as directing us to the healing of God's world and the coming birth of the new creation of which Paul speaks in Romans 8. The words, gestures, movement, music and all the elements of the eucharistic prayer proclaim what we want the whole world to become.

The words of the prayers point, even if not always explicitly, to the fulfillment of time and the process of change in which we now live. Thus the prayers, the actions, the positions of the congregation and its ministers, and the space itself all form an integrity with the liturgical text of the prayer. Where the integrity of the entire action is lacking or deficient, the Eucharist as symbol and sign for the community is correspondingly impaired.

The epiclesis, or prayer to the Holy Spirit, points to God's trans-forming work both in the gifts we offer and in the hearts and spirits of the baptized. Many eucharistic prayers articulate this "double epicle-sis" quite clearly:

> Lord, we pray that in your goodness and mercy your Holy Spirit may descend upon us, and upon these gifts, sanctifying them and showing them to be holy gifts for your holy people, the bread of life and the cup of salvation, the Body and Blood of your Son Jesus Christ. Grant that all who share this bread and cup may become one body and one spirit, a living sacrifice in Christ, to the praise of your Name.
>
> (Prayer D, Rite II, *Book of Common Prayer*)

The UCC Service of Word and Sacrament I prays very plainly and clearly: "We ask you to send your Holy Spirit on this bread and wine, on our gifts, and on us." The prayer continues with an explicit description of the work of the Spirit in the church that receives the gifts: "Strengthen your universal church that it may be the champion of peace and justice in all the world. Restore the earth with the grace that is able to make all things new." United Methodist Service of Word and Table I begs God to pour the Holy Spirit out on the bread and wine so that they may be the body and blood of Christ to those gathered, "that we may be for the world the body of Christ, redeemed by his blood."

Primavesi and Henderson rightly remind us that the epiclesis must be reclaimed by the community as the moment when "all ask for the Spirit; all are changed through union with the Spirit;" and all pray to be joined as one sharing in the life of Christ.[32] The Western church has sadly neglected this invocation to the Spirit in its eucharistic theology, and its strengthening in preaching, teaching, and ritual action could only strengthen the church. This prayer makes the explicit connection between God's action in transforming our gifts of bread and wine and our lives in the world, and our receiving the life of Jesus Christ in the symbols of bread and wine and in our selves and our whole spiritual and material world.

A doxology most appropriately ends the prayer by drawing the action of that particular Eucharist explicitly to the life of God now and in the world to come. The doxology thus functions as a concluding and summarizing prayer, which is also a reminder of the eschatological

fulfillment of each Eucharist and of the whole life of God's people on
earth.

Communion. After the concluding doxology and the Lord's Prayer,
which proclaims our petition to God to hallow God's name and bring
God's reign to earth, the bread is broken and the wine poured out, that
all may gather around one table to share in the banquet. The moment
of communion allows the sacrificial aspect of the Eucharist to be acted
out in perspective of its life-giving quality. As the mother's milk,
which is quite costly to the mother's body, gives life and nourishment
to the infant, an even more costly offering gives new life to humanity.

Both the life and the way in which it is given emphasize the corporate character of the Eucharist. "The gifts of God for the people of
God" is an invitation used in the Byzantine liturgy, now frequently
used in Western prayers. The Eucharist is acclaimed as the people's
nourishment, which continually remakes the baptized into the people
of God, which they are made in Baptism. Robinson speaks of the
Communion as the "great workshop of the new world,"[33] in which we
altogether, regardless of race, class, sex, age, receive the same bread
and wine and are nourished by the same Spirit with the same life of
Christ.

Both the gifts received and the way in which we all receive the
same bread and the same cup symbolize quite clearly the infinite value
and complete equality of each of us at God's table. The practical consequences are immense. The oneness of the eucharistic community
creates the radical interconnection of all members of God's household.
The obvious (if not well-practiced) implication of this community is
the abolition of distinctions based on color, class, sex, or any other
worldly distinction. All are equally dependent on God and equally
interdependent on each other. As the sharing at table is uncondition-
al, our interdependence and responsibility for each other is also uncon-
ditional. In practice, this raises ongoing questions for Christians about
how to share prayer and daily life together. The responses have ranged
from the creation of religious communities and communes to the utter
ignoring of shared Christian life in everyday reality.

Since the days of Paul in Corinth (1 Cor. 11–13), Christians have
been arguing about what difference their eucharistic communion
makes to their daily life. The only possible answer is that it makes an
absolute difference, even if we are not all ready to practice the sort of

everyday economic community outlined in Acts 4:32-35. The Eucharist makes us all responsible for spiritual and material care for all our brothers and sisters joined to us in this holy meal.

Each community and individual struggles with *how* to be responsible to one another in practical as well more abstract ways, not *if* we are to do so. It seems quite unlikely that any group of Christians will agree about how to carry out this eucharistic commission, but discussion and action are essential to any sort of Christian life. With such a vast array of social issues in the world, the Christian community can enrich the public discussion and strengthen itself for the opposition it will face through serious consideration about the connection between eucharistic communion and interconnection of people in the world.

The eucharistic banquet also offers us a model of the world we seek to bring into earthly reality. We have seen, not so many years ago, churches divided by race, where black and white would not share the gifts together. The church thus mirrored the sinful discrimination of society. God's call to the church, at the moment of communion, is to share the gifts together and then to go forth into the world to remake the world in Christ's name in the model of the eucharistic banquet, where all share at the table as one.

Dismissal. After Communion, a common prayer of thanksgiving, and usually a blessing, the congregation is dismissed. The most common dismissal in the early church was the deacon's "go in peace" to the people. These words had a practical effect of announcing the end of the Eucharist, but they also emphasized that the end of the service was the beginning of a renewed life. When Hippolytus described the first communion of the newly baptized, he writes that after all have communicated, "each hastens to do good works, to please God and live a good life. He is to devote himself to the Church, putting what he has been taught into practice and making progress in the service of God."[34]

Thus the dismissal is a significant ritual element of the eucharistic celebration. It directs the baptized into the practice of their eucharistic faith. It calls them to live the Gospel in their everyday lives and to anticipate the fullness of God's life actualized in the world. The dismissal proclaims to the congregation that "the end of worship here on earth is not at the Altar; the end is in the wide and wicked world. The end is in lives laid down as His life is laid down, for love that will not be denied."[35] The body and blood of Jesus are now one with the body and blood of the baptized, and they are to continue their Eucharist in the world, good in its creation and torn by human abuse, each commissioned to be Christ to the people among whom they live.

The Worshiping Community and the World. In John's Gospel, when Jesus dies on the cross, he cries out: "It is fulfilled *(tetelestai)*" (John 19:30). Jesus did not die, according to John, by accident or misadventure. He intended to offer himself as a sacrifice to God, knowing that God would accept his self-offering, and in accepting Jesus, all things would be drawn to God. In Jesus' death, the *telos* (purpose) of the incarnation would be fulfilled.

But Jesus does not simply die and then is taken down and buried. According to John, on this eve of the Passover Sabbath, Pilate orders the bodies to be removed from their crosses. One of the soldiers, seeing that Jesus appears to be dead, pierces his side with a spear. Blood and water, according to John, flows from his side; these things happened that the Scripture might be fulfilled (John 19:31-37).

From the days of the very early church, the blood and water were interpreted to be signs of the Baptism and Eucharist that Jesus left to his followers to make them into the church, the community that would continue Jesus' life and ministry in the world. From its very early days, the church has believed that Jesus' sacrifice on the cross immediately offered his followers Baptism into his death and resurrection and the nourishment of his sacrificial meal. The purpose of these great gifts, given at the painful and profane place, is to nourish Jesus' disciples in continuing his work of drawing all things to God.

To that mission, nourished at the Eucharist, we now turn.

6.

The World Becoming Itself
Liturgy and the Future

In Norway during the late 1800s, at the foot of the mountains of Berlevaag Fjord, lived two elderly ladies, Martine and Philippa, daughters of a dean and prophet who had founded a pious sect. "Its members," Isak Dinesen writes, "renounced the pleasures of this world, for the earth and all it held to them was but a kind of illusion, and the true reality was the New Jerusalem toward which they were longing." These two unmarried sisters lived together in the dean's old house, treasuring the memory of their father, offering hospitality to the dwindling number of their father's followers, and spending their time and slender funds in works of charity.

"Babette's Feast" is Dinesen's spare and sparkling tale of the celebratory banquet that their mysterious French maid-of-all-work, Babette, prepared for them to celebrate the dean's one-hundredth birthday anniversary. Through a series of events in the two elderly sisters' lives and their fleeting contacts with the world outside, Babette Hersant fled from Paris in 1871 to take refuge with them from the suppression of the Communards. Achilles Pain, Philippa's old singing master, sent her to Berlevaag. There the sisters gave her refuge, and she became their dedicated cook and maid.

For years Babette lived quietly with the two sisters, serving them. At first they feared she might be extravagant; instead she proved herself frugal and skilled in providing the most excellent and nourishing of food from the most modest of ingredients. Babette retained her dignity and distance; the sisters and indeed the believers and the whole town grew to respect and greatly appreciate this stoic and diligent woman.

After twelve years Babette received a letter informing her that the lottery ticket a friend in Paris had been annually renewing for her had won the ten-thousand-franc prize. Although the sisters feared that Babette would inform them that she was returning to France, instead she asked for one favor: to prepare a banquet, a real French dinner, to celebrate the dean's one-hundredth birthday anniversary. After much deliberation, with great trepidation about the fearful luxury and waste, the sisters consented.

In November Babette went away for ten days to order supplies from Paris. The next weeks saw increasing preparations. The brothers and sisters of the dean's sect vowed that they would come to the feast, but they would speak no word about the food or drink, because at the last day God would purify all sensuality from them, so that they would be able to concentrate on praise and thanksgiving to God.

That Sunday, twelve gathered for the feast. The twelve included General Loewenhielm, who had thirty years earlier abandoned his courtship of Martine to pursue his career in the army. When they had sat down at table and begun to drink the wine and eat the turtle soup, of a quality that astonished the General, they all began to talk freely about the Dean's life among them.

The General rose to speak about grace, which, when we believe we have refused it, is granted freely to us. As the evening progressed, the sisters and brothers had no specific memories, but recalled that it seemed that a heavenly light filled the rooms, and those present were able peacefully to move past those developments that divided them and return to an earlier unity. It seemed to them that time and eternity joined, the illusions of earth disappeared, and "they had seen the universe as it really was."

At the end of the meal, when the guests had departed into the moonlight toward their homes, the two sisters went to the kitchen to speak to the exhausted Babette. Martine and Philippa were astonished to learn that Babette had spent her ten thousand francs to provide this feast for them. But when they responded to her with pity, she replied that she had spent so much not for them but for herself because "I am a great artist!" Then Philippa, who had herself refused the opportunity to go to Paris and sing with Monsieur Pain, recognized the name of the Café Anglais of which Babette had been the chef. She echoed the words that Pain had once written to her of her own career: "'Yet this is not the end! . . . In Paradise you will be the great artist that God meant you to be! Ah!' she added, the tears streaming down her cheeks. 'Ah, how you will enchant the angels!'"[1]

Dinesen's sensitively and richly modeled story of Babette's feast, like all great literature, speaks to many aspects of our awareness, even those only partially conscious of the drama unfolding before us. The themes woven together include the relationship between time and eternity, earth and heaven, God and humanity, aspirations and limitations, the interconnections of people with each other, human belonging to the earth, the power of art and symbol, and the life-giving strength of hope and dedication.

Through the meal prepared by a great artist, the moment of epiphany—revelation of the connection of divine and earthly, the presence of grace here and now—comes even to narrow and rigid souls who would deny the present reality of God in the world in order to preserve themselves for a disembodied eternity. Babette's feast, freely given to them at great cost as well as deep fulfillment to Babette, opens their eyes and changes them into people who, at least for a time, are at one with themselves, each other, and the world. Dinesen reminds us that they will never lose that vision.

The tale also affirms the reality of the future fulfillment of our present experience of incompleteness and frustration, with the possibility of rare but sustaining moments of wholeness. Neither Babette nor the sisters pretend that everything is perfect right now; they do not deny the reality of the frustrations of their lives or their incompleteness. They affirm, however, that moments in this present age open up an infinite and deep reality that can burst forth if we give it the opportunity.

Eucharist and the Eschatological Ideal

Without trying to exaggerate the point, Dinesen created a spare but rich literary metaphor for the Eucharist. The Eucharist is itself the great feast, given to us at the greatest cost by Jesus, with the power within it to give us the experience of grace—the great vision of our communion with God, each other, and the world—and to offer us a glimpse of this world's true fulfillment in God. At the liturgy, we dramatize our symbolic imagery of what we believe God has created the world to be, and of what, by God's grace, we want this world to become. The liturgy thus expresses in its forms and actions both what, in God's revealing light, we want to become, and the directions in which we believe God is calling us to move.

What will become of me? Us? Does my life, our relationship as a community, our worship of God have any significance? Is it all just a flash in the pan, a "tale told by an idiot, full of sound and fury, signifying nothing?" (William Shakespeare, *Macbeth,* V, v, 26–28). People have responded differently to these questions over the millennia, as they do today.

Perhaps life is nothing more than a brief spark for each of us, an explosion of energy in the face of chaos. Some have held that the universe is a static reality in which individuals take their place. Others assert that each life now is a point on an unvarying continuum; still others describe time as consisting of infinite repetitive cycles, with human life after death as a continuation in a static eternity or an unending cycle of rebirths.

Another response is that the world is presently in a time of development or of conflict. The assumption is that the world's existence is purposeful. One version of this view is that the world is in a process of development, complex and perhaps painful, to a maturity only vaguely perceived now, and in which all creation will share. Another view of the purposeful world assumes that the universe is in a process of conflict between good and evil and is moving toward a time of final battle and definitive judgment by God, ushering in harmony between the world and God.[2]

Who am I in this world of God, creatures, earth, and sky? What difference do my life and work make? What happens when I die? Who or what cares about my life and death? Such fundamental human questions make eschatology an enduring human curiosity.

Eschatology is thus of vital importance in eucharistic theology. The Greek word *eschaton* means "end" or "last" things or times. In the earlier layers of biblical material, the last things referred to God's promise of the land to Abraham and his descendants, his descendants' inheritance of the land, God's judgment of the people for their disobedience, and God's pledge of future restoration. This prophetic eschatology, as Richard H. Heirs noted, becomes mixed with later apocalyptic eschatology. Apocalyptic eschatology assumes that the world was so dominated by evil that only the immediate, direct intervention of God could free the faithful and establish God's reign of justice and peace on earth.[3]

Thus the term *eschatology* is, in theological usage, a very broad one, which can indicate a wide variety of interpretations of the future of creation, from a future creation through human action in obedience to God to a definition of the "end time" as one imposed on a passive humanity through God's immediate intervention. Eschatology also can encompass everything from the individual "end" of heaven, purgatory, or hell, to the end of the world's or the universe's time.[4]

The notion of eschatology also includes a dimension that C. H. Dodd discussed in his work on Jesus' parables about the reign of God. In Jesus' announcement of the reign of God, the end of time is present, as well as being yet-to-come. Dodd interprets Jesus' parables and sayings as indicating that Jesus did not expect an apocalyptic fulfillment of the end time but insisted that he already contained the beginning of the end of time. This realized eschatology of Jesus' ministry represented "the impact upon this world of the 'powers of the world to come' in a series of events, unprecedented and unrepeatable, now in actual progress."[5]

Dominic Crossan distinguishes apocalyptic eschatology, which asserts that God has given the chosen community alone a secret revelation about the immediate end of time to restore peace and justice, from sapiential eschatology, which he claims is Jesus' own message, signifying that God has given everyone that wisdom to live here and now in the world in such a way that "God's power, rule, and dominion are evidently present to all observers."[6]

These varied interpretations remind us not only of the long history of eschatology but of its contemporary interest. Every perspective I have named lives on in contemporary Christianity, from those Christians who expect imminent Armageddon, to the ones who believe that the essence of the Christian life is to make this world a better place.[7]

How does our eschatology form our liturgy? And how does liturgy shape our eschatology? Answers are diverse in the Christian tradition, as one might expect. But whatever the perspective, every Eucharist expresses an eschatological perspective. The second-century Didache expresses the continuing expectation of the return of the Messiah. The Western medieval Mass looks forward to the Last Judgment and the end of time. The Liturgy of John Chrysostom contains the elements of the present and future life with God of the community, but also articulates in word and gesture that the moment of the liturgy is an anticipation in time and space of the fullness of time yet to come. In the U.S. Free Church tradition, the focus becomes individualized and personalized, centering on myself and on my present and future life with Jesus.

The root of a liturgical eschatological perspective is that God created the world, including humans, imperfect and unfinished, yet intended to and yearning to be more. We and our world are not what we ought to be, what God created us to be, and at the same time, we can move closer to or further from what we are able to be. Eschatology functions thus both as the burr under the saddle and the ideal of what we want to be. It asserts that we are not yet in the fullness of God's reign and that our life, as a part of the world, is in the process of being directed and of moving toward that fullness.

God does not abandon the world to its condition of failed aspirations and possibilities but pledges that the world will become, in God's way and time, what it was created to be. Our human history is thus to be interpreted, as Don E. Saliers notes, "as God's new covenant promises for the future of the world."[8] The Christian is thus a creature of hope, even while not seeing clearly how God's creative will can be realized in the world. Can there be any moments, times, or places that reassure us, speak to us of a promise being realized in us, show us a transformation happening, or at least suggest what this transformation might look like? How does an eschatological perspective become part of the Christian community's life?

Scriptures, religious traditions, and theological speculations are important. They express and explain the hopes and expectations of the religious community about its origins, daily life, and purpose in the universe. Equally vital to the community are those times and places when the world seems to break open with the revealing of what the world ought to be. We humans can from time to time glimpse the way the world was made to be. "Babette's Feast" offers a concise and elegant expression of one of those illuminating moments. These instants of hope incarnate in our time and space the world as God made it to be.

Both cognitive expression and the rich events of life that reveal our hope to come share in the tension and fragility of our present life. Eschatology is not the description of an inexorable march to cosmic perfection, whatever that might be, but a tense and varied drama, filled with uncertainty, choices, good, and evil. The Christian is convinced that for those whom God loves, all things work together for good (Rom. 8:28). But *how* this happens, or why humans act and respond to God and each other in particular ways and contexts, is often unclear to us and at best fragmentary and seen "as in a glass darkly" (1 Cor. 13:12). A constant reality in our Christian life is tension and uncertainty, which live in us side by side with confidence and hope of our entering into God's realm on earth.[9]

For the Christian community, the liturgy embodies the connection between bright ideal and compromised reality, future hope and present realities, the new creation and our life being transformed. Liturgy functions as the "arc to link the bitter world . . . to altar and song of praise."[10] The connecting action of the liturgy empowers the community in illuminating and expressing the experience of the world, which often seems disturbed, in conflict with ideals, or even overtly evil, within the context of the vision of God's new creation. Glimmers of hope, visions of what might be, acknowledgment of frustration, identification of paths by which one might move forward: all are part of the Christian liturgy.

Our vision of the future for which God has created the universe and our present and future in that universe are crucial to our corporate worship. One may interpret the meaning of our hope in various ways, but that eschatological bedrock is central to the Christian faith and is the foundation of all liturgy. Liturgy expresses, here and now, how we anticipate that hope here and now and act accordingly in our world here and now.

What Does God Want the World to Become?

Our liturgy is the symbolic action expressing the intersection of what we are and what we hope to become. Rowan Williams suggests that "we read the Prayer Book as setting out within the context of worship a vision of the Christian commonwealth, a kind of model of the relations which would have to prevail in a society for the members of the society to say their prayers honestly."[11] Such a model of the human commonwealth offers a divine critique and positive guide for the recreation of human society in this world.

At the same time, the liturgy also shows us the vision of the reign of God, in which the whole of creation is united in God. The Eucharist is the drama of the "heavenly banquet where God is our host. . . . [T]he whole delight of the gathering is the limitless and marvelous generosity of the Host."[12] Our eschatology does not culminate in sanctified human effort but in God's gift of grace in bringing all things to their fulfillment.

Before we explore how this eschatological aspect of liturgy can be realized in the life of a community, a great, simple, and basic truth needs to be openly acknowledged. Liturgy is a divine and human intersection. God's actions are praised, received more deeply into our lives as a community and individually, and interpreted by us. God is present and active in our assembly and our worship, but we humans construct the liturgy and enact it, guided by our biblical and historical encounters with God.

Thus like any other human creation, perhaps especially one so near to the heart of our human condition, liturgy can be frustratingly short of what it is created to be. "The gap between this reality that is offered, and what our social body is capable of receiving is sometimes excruciating."[13] We humans can be, as the Corinthian Christians were in Paul's day, contentious and divisive in the very liturgy that is a pledge and foretaste of unity in God. Confession of sin can be a perfunctory and superficial muttering, the kiss of peace either ignored or an opportunity for chatty gossip, the prayers of the people a time for political or personal vindictiveness, and the sharing of bread and wine at the altar denied by greedy and vicious treatment of each other in the marketplace or at home.

The reality of corporate and individual shortcomings and deliberate evil can "contradict or deny"[14] the intention of liturgy, the healing and hopeful sign of the world being reconciled to God. Liturgy is both God's gracious symbol of transformation and also under God's judgment as one more venue in which foolish and sinful humanity can distort or refuse God's promises. Those who form liturgies and those who participate in them need always to be reexamining how the liturgies can better call us back from our wanderings. Part of every community and individual life includes an ongoing honest self-examination about the existential truthfulness of its liturgy and life. The confession of sin, promise of amendment, and absolution are necessary not only for life outside the liturgy, but for what we do within our worship, and for our failure to live up to grace offered us in our liturgy.

Acknowledging that our liturgy is itself imperfect as we form and celebrate it in our communities, how do we want our liturgy to express God's future for us and with us? How does the liturgy form, encourage, respond, and guide us? It reminds, motivates, and symbolically embodies for us both God's fullness of time and our growth and struggle toward it. At the same time it roots us in God's creative love, our cosmic and human past, all living reality that moves dynamically toward its fullness. Thus liturgy points us to the fullness of God's reign; directs us in the process of actualizing, albeit imperfectly, God's realm on earth; and anticipates the fullness of life rooted in but beyond our present experience.

The shape of the liturgy embodies this multidimensional activity. Even a sketch of the action of the Eucharist points to its power to nurture hope and cultivate transforming grace in our lives.

Gathering. The Christian community gathers together in a common building around one altar/table as one people. The unity does not destroy the multiplicity of people, gifts, resources, sins, blessings, and so forth. Those differences are to be exercised in the service of the common good, the community of believers in which all are of infinite value, with the right to be safe, supported, protected, freed to exercise their gifts in the community, fed, clothed, and nurtured in relationship with God, each other, and the whole cosmos.

The community of worshipers, gathered together with different gifts and common rights and responsibilities, symbolically embodies the world as it will be in the fullness of time, and the world as God expects us to be trying now to live. Regardless of what political agenda we embrace, our worship of God calls us to work for a world of perfect intercommunion, and to work for it now. The liturgy is God's imperative and invitation to transform this world into one in which all people are equal in their life in the world as they are in the liturgy. A community in which a third of the children go hungry violates the essence of liturgical worship, sharing the bread and wine through which Christ gives us life.

What of order in the liturgy, or the role so beloved of us in the more liturgical traditions? Ultimately, God is the font of creative life and love, maker of order and giver of freedom. But in the interim, human beings are rightly designated, formally or informally by the community, to make order; ceremonies and rites are devised to embody the community's faith, to facilitate everyone's participation, and to guide the community in the worship of God and service of God's world. As Gordon Lathrop notes, order is a gift, especially for those whose lives are "painful and chaotic," because it is a "social event" that embodies an ordered society in a wider ordered world.[15] Liturgical order empowers us to imagine, Lathrop continues, what the world might become.[16]

Order is a sine qua non of any community life. It may be the undeviating order of elaborate hierarchy, or the free-flowing order of tribal societies in which everyone cooperates in well-understood but barely articulated ways for the common good. Order may exist in many ways, but some corporately accepted boundaries and ways of acting together are essential to any society's continuing existence. Only with order can we exercise our free choice, hear and be heard, speak and be spoken to, or engage in any of the interactions of ordinary life.

Order is a fine balance of the community boundaries and patterns that encourage and allow development but also provide the dependable support of everyone's life. The liturgical order of the gathered community expresses this balance in the world we await and the world we are making through God's grace on earth. It may be embodied in Solemn Pontifical Mass at St. Peter's Basilica in Rome or the excitement of the midsummer revival at Mesquite Road Bible Baptist Church. Each worshiping community has its liturgical order, with its roles and actions expressing its hopes and desires for this life and the life to come. The interconnection of different roles and functions, patterns of time, motions and gestures, and the dynamic of the liturgy itself all express the order and freedom of life together that we need, strive for, and anticipate.

The rhythm and movement of the liturgy—from gathering to dismissal—draws participants into a pattern of life that embodies the hope for the way we might grow to live our present-day lives and also anticipate our future with God. In a very small and informal worshiping community, the roles and actions may be very simple, barely differentiated, and shared easily. In a larger group, the actions may be more elaborate and ritualized. In any situation, the liturgy works to draw us together to transform us, to move and to strengthen us in the world God wants this to be, as we await God's time of fulfillment for all of us.

The Action. We hear God's word and have been gathered through God's gracious love. We pray and reflect on this word—what it means in transforming us and our world. We pray for the world, for the church, and for all our varied needs and concerns. We confess, repent, and reconcile with God and one another, acting in our own lives the hope we have for the whole world in God's grace. We then offer ourselves and our world to God, we ourselves being God's gifts to the world. God acts in the eucharistic prayer to receive these gifts, through the power of the Holy Spirit transforming the bread and wine into the symbolic bearers of divine life for us, and deepening the transforming power of the Spirit so that we might live into our baptismal vocation as disciples. In the radical equality of the eucharistic banquet, we share in the symbols of new life, give thanks, and are sent forth to live our eucharistic life in the world.

The Episcopal *Book of Common Prayer* on the whole is clear, if general, in its vision of what this world is to be. In the Postcommunion Prayer (which of course must be interpreted in context of the Baptismal Covenant, pp. 304–5), the congregation is commissioned to go into the world in peace "to love and serve you, in gladness and singleness of heart" (p. 365). In Eucharistic Prayer C, the priest prays in the community's name, "Make us one body, one spirit in Christ, that we may worthily serve the world in his name" (p. 372). What will this world look like? How do we serve God in transforming the world?

The Prayers of the People (for example, Form I on pp. 383–85) tend to have the most specific imaging of the world here and now as we anticipate God's order for it. We pray for religious and political harmony, conservation of the earth, safe travel for people, help for all in need, deliverance from "danger, violence, oppression, and degradation." The Prayers for the Social Order (pp. 823-27) and for the Natural Order (pp. 827-28), which can be used on any occasion, offer a more specific vision of social transformation, both of what we hope for and how we humans need to change ourselves and to change the world in Christ's name.

The *Book of Worship* of the United Church of Christ contains some prayers that not only express a vision of what the world is to become, but how God expects us to change to bring about this renewal. The congregation prays for forgiveness in Christmastide, because "we tolerate hatred, violence, and injustice in the world you love so well that you sent the child Jesus, begotten from your own being" (p. 484). On Easter, the congregation prays that God will "free us to risk ourselves in the struggle for justice and peace that we may be your partners in restoring all creation to your will" (p. 497).

In the prayers of the community for the time after Pentecost, the diversity of the church is upheld as a cause of rejoicing. "We thank you that we count as our brothers and sisters in Christ people of all races, tongues, and nations. From the villages of India to the mountains of Peru, from the cities of Russia to the plains of Canada, your name is praised" (p. 507). These examples suggest how, within the more general forms used by the worshiping community, we can articulate very specific visions of our behavior in moving toward the world order God intends for us.

Our worship and our eucharistic life are authentic only if we are ourselves the arc connecting the altar and the world, worship in the church with life on the street. Thus the pattern of worship is vital in enacting the mode of radical transformation we seek for the world. Liturgical worship, as Don Saliers noted, "forms and expresses dispositions belonging to a way of life before God in relation to our neighbor."[17] Liturgy teaches us through words and actions how to live in our world.

Our dispositions express themselves in the worship and continue in our life in the world. The behavior of the worshipers expresses the way of life Christians seek always—the friendliness of the greeters, the cooperation of the worshipers in finding a place, singing together, the shared reverence and prayerfulness, earnest listening to the Word, friendly and forgiving exchange of the peace, generous giving, mutually respectful and equal sharing of the gifts, and energized return to the world. Such attitudes and actions speak eloquently of the power of the Spirit to transform us and our world.

Members of a congregation that worships in such ways treat each other as sister and brother, worthy of respect and reconciliation. God's creative love and intention for the world are always the guide and the spur for its corporate and individual activity in the world. Such are the communities that encourage people openly to acknowledge that the Eucharist calls us to live in radically new ways, predicated on a call for a radical justice in the world. "The holy Eucharist is for those who have an intimate sharing fellowship which prompts them to share the material wealth also with those with whom they communicate."[18]

Not everyone who shares the eucharistic meal will live out that insight in the same way or with the same fervor, but all will live by it and compare their own and their congregation's life by such ideals.

These Christians are on the picket line, demanding justice, and in boardrooms, striving for more justice and equity among people. People who communicate at the same altar work on projects that benefit their sisters and brothers because they have eaten at the same table and feel these bonds of life in Christ to be more real and true than even those of their family.

Such Christians don't necessarily literally give everything away, but they do live as though everything, including life, is a gift God gives us to share. In private and public ways, they share their time, talent, and goods. Their homes are places of honest sharing and welcome for friends and strangers; their work and play gives them pleasure and contributes to others' lives. They root out bitterness in their relations with others and encourage the good.

Those who are nourished at the same table acknowledge readily that the ways of the world are not always God's ways. Individual efforts, they know, are not always enough. Just as in the Eucharist, we are a community that prays together in mind and body, so for the world to become fully God's world, we must become God's community and transform our community of life.

All of our systems—educational, legal, financial, medical, social— have to be transformed in light of God's justice and love. Sometimes our baptismal commission into the world moves us to focus on transforming ourselves and our attitudes, and other times we acknowledge more directly that our worldly liturgy is part of the varied interconnected systems that nourish, shape, free, and sometimes impede us. Our Sunday liturgy shapes and enlivens this daily work of God's transforming grace through us.

We can, of course, experience quite the opposite way of enacting worship. The greeters can be hostile or neglecting; prayers can be casual or interrupted by coughs, squirms, or mutters; people can sit slumped in pews or stare coldly away from the clergy or the other parishioners; the offerings can be meanly or grudgingly given; communion can be a shoving match to see who gets there first; and the race out of church can be dangerous to your health.

One may even find liturgies that are much more decorous and polite but are focused on the congregation and various people's special abilities, rather than worship or consideration for one another. When a church is in conflict, often one will see that conflict acted out in the liturgy—some people won't speak to each other, parishioners won't receive communion from a particular clergy person, and people's anger echoes in prayers or readings. I have seen people turn their backs to each other at the exchange of the Peace and have heard others deliberately interrupt the singing of the community.

Sometimes people are quite reflective and aware of the connections between the liturgical drama and the life of the world. They can articulate their awareness that sharing the food and drink of life at the eucharistic banquet connects us in a web of divine interdependence that makes us responsible to each other to share earthly food and goods, as well as the life of the Spirit of prayer, hope, love, and justice. The offerings of bread and wine, labor and play, human life and relationships—all are the raw material of the Eucharist and are given form and direction for God's people living in the world.

As we worship God in our liturgies, we experience the continuing conversation that can move us from a halfhearted awareness of our prayer and an unwillingness to behave differently in the world to a developing centeredness in our relationship with God and openness to change our lives so that God's world may grow among us. In worship, the indifferent may become more ready to hear and act, those who "act out" their own disappointment and angers are invited to heal and change, and those who are intent on God's purposes are strengthened and encouraged to pray and work for God's new world. We may change, fall, and return, but our consistent sharing in the liturgy keeps us focused on who God is, who we are, and what we want ourselves and our world to be. It opens us to transformation in God's life.

Wholehearted participation in the liturgy does not produce uniform politics, education, or social systems. However, the community action of the liturgy does reaffirm and strengthen us in making a world in which oppression, greed, resentment, anger, and revenge are uprooted and replaced by peace, justice, hope, and love. We learn and are consistently reinforced in a new pattern of life, which teaches us to act on earth as we would in the very presence of God. Our liturgy is our teacher, our guide, and our anchor in this process. At worship we "remember the Lord until he comes," not so that we will sit around dreaming, but in order to learn to live in the power of Jesus' life in the reign of God on earth and in heaven. Our liturgies give us hope *in* the present life *for* the present life. We are nourished and strengthened to love and labor in the present for its betterment and to make the future even more fully the realm of God than is the present.

Hope for the Future

But do we really await any future after death? Our liturgy models justice and symbolizes the reign of God on earth. What does our liturgy say about a life to come, a fulfillment of God's reign in the world that transcends our experience of time and space, a hope of heaven interconnected with our hope for earth?

Colleen McDannell and Bernhard Lang note that today theology primarily either focuses on this life and refuses to discuss a life to come or reduces eternal life to a symbol dissociated from the substance of the theology. Alternatively, it may turn to a fundamentalist theology that centers on either the millennium or anthropomorphic sentimentalized pictures of a future life in heaven.[19] These theological realities affect profoundly the way liturgies are prayed, shaped, and interpreted, and they underscore the significance of the liturgical insistence that the present, the hope of the earthly future, and the expectation of eternal life are all integrally interconnected.

Our liturgies still contain references to eternal life; as has always been true, these references generally avoid specificity, but rather sparsely use biblical imagery, while insisting that God created this world for a present and future with God. For example, in its ordinary Sunday liturgy, the United Church of Christ's *Book of Worship* is very frugal in references to a life other than this present one. In its Service of Holy Communion I, in Option A, the community affirms its faith in "awaiting Christ's return in victory." In the epiclesis, we ask God to "restore the earth with your grace that is able to make all things new." In Option B, the community prays that we may "remain faithful in love and hope until the perfect feast with our exalted Savior in the eternal joy of your heavenly realm."[20]

In the Service of Word and Sacrament II, Option B, in the Eucharistic Prayer, the pastor introduces the acclamation by saying, "We remember Christ's promise not to drink of the fruit of the vine again until the heavenly banquet at the close of history, and we say boldly what we believe . . . " (p.71).

In the service of Thanksgiving for One Who Has Died, at the procession various scriptural references to eternal life with God are cited. The greeting speaks at length of the congregation's response to death and mortality and "commends to God with thanksgiving the life of " the deceased (p. 372). The recurring theme is that nothing "will be able to separate us from the love of Christ Jesus our Lord"(p. 375). Option B of the Prayers of Intercession speaks of the deceased entering the home "where all your people gather in peace." The leader prays that eventually all of us may "rejoice together in the heavenly family where Jesus Christ reigns with you and the Holy Spirit" (p. 377). The commendation offers a choice of a contemporary prayer that entrusts the deceased to God, or a reformulation of the committal prayer from the *Book of Common Prayer,* which asks God to receive the deceased "into the arms of your mercy, into the blessed rest of everlasting peace, and into the company of the saints in light" (p. 381).

In the Episcopal Church's *Book of Common Prayer,* similar descriptions of human life after death are offered: sparse affirmations of faith are made. The Nicene Creed is required at the Sunday Eucharist, in either rite. "We look for the resurrection of the dead, and the life of the world to come" (p. 327, 359). In the Prayers of the People of Rite I, the last petition asks God for grace to "follow the good example of _____ and of all thy saints, that with them we may be partakers of thy heavenly kingdom" (p. 330). All the various Prayers of the People suggested for Rite II either pray that we may share eternal life with the saints, or pray for those who have died, that they may partake of life eternal. The Absolution after the Confession offers the same typically Anglican combination of moral exhortation and faith in eternal life: "pardon and deliver you from all your sins, confirm and strengthen you in all goodness, and bring you to everlasting life" (pp. 332–60).

In the Eucharistic Prayer of Rite One, the priest prays that "we may be filled with thy grace and heavenly benediction, and made one body with him, that he may dwell in us and we in him" (p. 336). Prayer A of Rite II, in the invoking of the Holy Spirit over the people, prays that the people may receive the sacrament faithfully, serve God in "unity, constancy and peace; and at the last day, bring us with all your saints into the joy of your eternal kingdom" (p. 363). The same theme is repeated in the same place in the Eucharistic Prayers B and D (p. 369, 374, 375).

The Prayer of Humble Access begs that "we may evermore dwell in him and he in us" (p. 337). One of the Words of Administration of Holy Communion affirms, "The Body (Blood) of our Lord Jesus Christ keep you in everlasting life," and another is "the Body of Christ, the bread of heaven. The Blood of Christ, the cup of salvation" (p. 338, 365). The Post-Communion Prayer incorporates two related themes with regard to eternal life: "that we are very members incorporate in the mystical body of all faithful people, and are also heirs, through hope, of thy everlasting kingdom." The next petition of the prayer is that by God's grace, "we may continue in that holy fellowship, and do all such good works as thou has prepared for us to walk in" (p. 336, 339).

The Burial Office, which normally is in context of a Eucharist, is filled with numerous biblical and liturgical references to the promise of the deceased continuing life in the resurrection of Christ, as part of the "one communion and fellowship, in the mystical body of thy son Christ our Lord" (p. 480). Humanity living on earth is "still in our pilgrimage, walking by faith" (p. 481). The connection is made between the Eucharist, which is the earthly foretaste, and the heavenly banquet, which the faithful inherit. The eternal kingdom of God is described as that place "where there is no death, neither sorrow nor crying, but the fullness of joy with all thy saints" (p. 482, 498). Those who celebrate the funeral Eucharist pray that they may join on the last day with the deceased to be "partakers of the inheritance with the saints in light" (p. 487).

Our liturgies insistently weave together Christian behavior on earth and the entrance into God's eternal realm. The communal element is also pronounced; the relationship is not between God and the believer as an isolated individual of faith, but between God and the believer as a member of Jesus' community, the body of Christ, those baptized into Jesus' life, death, and resurrection, with all the saints, sharing with the angels in the light of God's eternal kingdom. Other Christian traditions' liturgies, with varying emphases, also focus on the relationship of the believer in the community with God and the connection between actions in this life and eternal life.

Certain elements are rather minimally present. They include the place in our Christian life and death of the struggle to realize God's realm imperfectly but truly on earth and the cosmic dimension of the eternal kingdom of God within which we live and die. The cosmic biblical themes of John 12:32; Romans 8:18-39; and 1 Corinthians 15:20-28 are not yet fully incorporated even into contemporary liturgical expressions of an eschatological faith. What, for instance, becomes of the earth in the fulfillment of the kingdom/reign of God? What is the place of animals, plants, rocks, and earth, in the fullness of God's reign?

Psalms are full of references to the creatures of the earth welcoming God to rule the earth (for example, 96, 99, 148, 150, and Pauline theology (for example, Rom. 8, Eph. 1, Colossians), which includes all creation in God's reign, makes a place for all creatures. The movement called "creation theology," process theology, and the work of Pierre Teilhard de Chardin have had very limited influence on the liturgy of the church. Worship is primarily concerned with humanity and its relationship with God; most often creation is a backdrop for the action of God with humanity, assisted by angels. Our liturgies do not yet adequately express the profoundly universal character of God's reign here and now and at the end time. Humanity's priesthood on behalf of creation; the relationship of all creation with God; the interconnection of all creatures, of planets, solar systems, and galaxies; good and evil, aspiration and frustration in all creatures; all these aspects are implicit in the eucharistic drama, but not yet adequately expressed in our churches' eucharistic liturgies.

Different cosmically aware theologies of the twentieth century bring into the mainstream of Christian reflection the interconnection of God with humanity as a part of a complex web of life. The developing field called "ecotheology" will enrich our understandings of past, present, and future of the world in God.[21] Only as we incorporate into our faith an awareness of all the cosmos as God's, in living relation to God, will we be able to express the interconnection of our present behavior, our transforming of the world through our present actions, and the ultimate future of the cosmos.

Teilhard de Chardin has provided the most comprehensive effort to connect an evolutionary perspective on the universe with the effects of human behavior, culture, and education. Teilhard is not afraid to acknowledge the death of the cosmos, just as he admits the death of individuals. But equally important as death is the life in which we participate as members of God's world. All our world's efforts in the sharing of life move us toward an end of time that is also a telos, a fulfillment. We do not exist as a bad cosmic joke, but are empowered as living creatures to change our present as a part of our movement toward the future of our world in God.[22]

Any contemporary eucharistic theology that seeks to offer us a perspective for present and future would need to combine our scientific perspectives with the deep and ancient symbols of faith that give us hope for the future. We are growing in our ability to articulate our awareness that a Christian life that is authentic to the Gospels cares and acts to be and do good in ourselves in regard to the whole world around us, from our most immediate contacts to the edges of space. The ways in which we act and the intensity we feel may differ, but the cosmos is our moral and spiritual home, in and through the God who is our beginning and our end.

The Eucharist and the Eschaton. Geoffrey Wainwright identifies six aspects of eschatological concern in the Eucharist: "Eschatology contains a polarity of the 'already' and the 'not yet' . . . concerns the individual in community . . . implies both a divine gift and a human appropriation . . . embraces the material and the spiritual . . . is universal in scope . . . allows progress in the establishment of the kingdom . . . involves a moment of judgment and renewal."[23]

These elements are normative and constitutive of the eucharistic action of a Christian community, although different elements will be emphasized in various liturgies of various periods and places. The Eucharist is not simply a symbol of a past event, an action to comfort believers in the present, a model of the sort of life the Gospel calls us to lead in the world, a promise and pledge of hope for ourselves and for our world. The Eucharist is an infinitely richer symbol for our present and our future.

Peoples and nations will shape worship differently;[24] even a quick look at our past reminds us that over the centuries Christians have been comforted and challenged by varying aspects of the vision of God's realm. The challenge over the ages to our liturgy has been to hold together the complex interweaving of God's revealing and our perceiving the multidimensional reality of God's reign among us on earth and in heaven.

Isak Dinesen wrote of "Babette's Feast": "The moment of epiphany when time and eternity, human art and divine creativity together met to illumine each other so that the human participants might grasp the true oneness in God of all creation." Teilhard, on an expedition in China's Ordos desert in August of 1923, lacking the bread and wine for mass, wrote a meditation about the dynamic presence of Christ in the cosmos, as sacramentalized for us in the Eucharist.

In the dry August heat of the desert, on the feast of the Transfiguration, Teilhard reflected on the radiating power of God's love in the whole physical world of which we are one part. Although Chardin is careful to distinguish the sacramental presence of Christ from its extension in the entire universe, he also identifies the intrinsic connection of the incarnate Christ, the eucharistic Christ, and the cosmic Christ. Because God's creative love became flesh in our world, the entire material universe is now included within God's life.[25]

The isolated Teilhard begins with the reflection that, not having the symbols of bread and wine, he will rise to "the pure majesty of the real itself; I, your priest, will make the whole earth my altar and on it will offer you all the labours and sufferings of the world."[26] He offers the whole creation, the "restless multitude," everything that will live, grow, diminish, or die. He utters his conviction that in the depths of the material universe is a deep hallowing desire that moves creation toward convergence, unity in love with the divine.

Power and Word were in the beginning, he asserts. Fire existed before all else, giving warmth and life into creation. God, Teilhard affirms, is the milieu in which the cosmos comes into being and grows into its completion. His prayer over the creation is that God's Word and Power transfigure the world. "Remould it, rectify it, recast it down to the depths from which it springs." Over every living thing: "This is my body." Over every death-force: "This is my blood."[27]

The metaphor that Teilhard uses to express this cosmic ongoing transformation is continuation of the never-ending birth of the Word of God into the world. For him, the incarnation of God in Jesus necessarily includes all matter in the life of the incarnate Christ. Consequently, all matter is henceforth connected with God in an unending process of movement toward fulfillment in God. Our human evolution is one mere particle of the cosmos' journey to God. In this sense, the world is God's flesh. Such a relationship does not assimilate everything into God, nor make God totally accessible to us, nor reduce us to passivity. Instead, he concludes, we respond to the Spirit who lures us forward to deeper and richer connections with the fullness of God.

The transforming work of fire is to "lay hold on me and absorb me." By this Teilhard means a renewal of each of us who is a "microcosm" of the Incarnation. For this renewal, we reach out to the fiery bread that binds us to the body of Christ, to lead us to heights where we would never choose to go. At the same time, we drink of the chalice, through which we die to all our grasping and our desire for advancement, for ourselves, and even for humanity.

After the universal consecration and communion, we pray that Jesus, teacher, friend, brother, also is the risen Sovereign of the universe, to whom we can surrender and be transformed. This communion will bring us to "that central point where the heart of the world is caught in the descending radiance of the heart of God." Through this communion we are energized and sent forth into the world having been formed in purity and charity, with a "vigorous determination that all of us together shall break open the doors of life." Finally we are given by God, in parting from this Mass over the world, a "blessed desire to go on advancing, discovering, fashioning and experiencing the world so as to penetrate ever further and further into [ourselves]."[28]

Teilhard's "Mass on the World," like Dinesen's "Babette's Feast," expresses in literary form the epiphanic opening of the world to those who would see and are willing to allow their lives to be transformed to the good. Dinesen focuses on the moment of epiphany, when time and eternity meet in an earthly event and for the willing participants the many dimensions of life in God are made clear. Teilhard articulates in eucharistic symbolic action the process of our continuing enfolding into God's reality, our transformation in context of the transformation of matter in the power of divine love. For both Dinesen and Teilhard, the dimensions of all creation's sharing in and expressing God's life are both present and eternal. Our own participation through the liturgy in the dynamic of this divine life roots us in the present, guiding and moving us into the future that we are laboring to make with God.

The unifying dimension of eschatology in the liturgy celebrates the interconnection of all our creation in God's gracious time-embracing eternity. All are interwoven in God's unbounded and unending activity: the past we remember, the todays of our present lives, the future we are striving to make in our world, and God's gracious shaping of maturity to our world. The Eucharist expresses the bedrock and the horizons of our faith, that our prayers and our work, our hopes and our dreams, our labors and our play, are all living and active parts of the pulsating life of God's creation, made one through Jesus the divine Wisdom, by the power of the Spirit, who brooded over the world at the beginning and draws it toward its fullness in the cosmic power of God's love.

Epilogue

"Hope that is seen is not hope," wrote Paul the apostle. If he was right, our age has much reason to hope. Little tangible evidence in our world reassures us about our future and offers us hope. Our days seem characterized by social unrest, ever-fragmenting civil wars, the growth of mean-spiritedness in the ways we treat one another, and an increasing atmosphere of conviction that we can do nothing to change things. Life is never all we hope for, history suggests, but some generations seem more aware than others of the earth's problems and the weight to give our difficulties. Ours seems highly disenchanted.

Today in North America we live in an overtly pluralistic culture, in which there are no common myths about beliefs and aspirations for the nation or individuals. Public symbols, political or religious leadership, Jewish or Christian values—all seem held in disrepute or at best not to receive common allegiance. Consumerism appears to be our one common value, with the increasing purchase of goods the means of control humans feel over their world, and individual material prosperity the only shared hope, no matter how fleeting. The vulgarity, materialism, rootlessness, and anti-intellectualism of American society have come to fruition in a world in which there seem to be no countervailing voices.[1]

In this postmodern world, the experiences of random shootings, fragmenting nations, competing value systems, and the unraveling of familiar institutions produce unease, even when people may approve of aspects of some changes. Increasingly people seek rootedness, belonging, some sense of hope for themselves and for the world's future.[2] In such a fragile society, we can be agents of hope if we shape, prepare, and celebrate our liturgies within the matrix of our baptismal faith, rooted and grounded in God.[3]

Do we wish to feel and know who we are? The repeated actions of the Eucharist, ever rooted in the past, ever new and ever renewing, direct us to our own future and that of our world with God. In the Eucharist, we receive and respond to God's gift to us. In the Eucharist, through our prayers, our actions, our connections with each other, our world, and with God, we affirm that the divine creative power that made us upholds, sustains, and nurtures us and our universe, teaches us how to live, and draws us into the future of the world more deeply than we can imagine.

As God's people, surrounding the altar in worship, we affirm the goodness of creation, the reality of sin, our experience of God's love and involvement for us and for our world. By our participation we choose hope over despair, transformation by God's energy rather than surrender to evil and inertia, and community among God's people rather than isolation with our own self and our efforts. We share the eucharistic feast in order that we may live in the world as those who see Christ's love present in and transforming the world and as those who share in Christ's transforming life.

Our liturgy reminds us that our identity is not as isolated individuals, but as members of God's universe; our hope is not individual or merely for our span of earthly life alone, but for the whole world, all over the globe and through its whole history. Most crucially, in our worship through the ever-living Spirit of God—in which everything that is made offers itself and is offered to God—works in all of us to bring us to a closer life in God.

In our liturgy, we worshipers experience prayer, listening, offering, sharing the blessed bread and wine, and being sent into the world to spread the good news by word and deed. In our liturgy we embody, again and again, in immeasurable times and places, that "great multitude that no one could count, from every nation, from all tribes and peoples and languages, standing before the throne and before the Lamb" (Rev. 7:9). We worship in faith and hope, "as in a glass darkly" (1 Cor. 13:12), unsure just what the fulfillment of God's promise to the world will look and feel like yet certain that the creative, reconciling, and all-holy God will renew the heavens and the earth to embrace all creation into an infinite life and love that surpasses all human knowing.

Notes

1. The Liturgy as Sacred Drama: Its Shape and Movement

1. Gregory Dix, *The Shape of the Liturgy* (London: Dacre, 1945, 1975), xviii.

2. Paul Avis, *Anglicanism and the Christian Church* (Minneapolis: Fortress, 1989), 8–20; Gregory Dix, *The Shape of the Liturgy,* 743–52; Anne Primavesi and Jennifer Henderson, *Our God Has No Favourites* (Tunbridge Wells, Eng.: Burns & Oates, 1989), 1–13; Aiden Kavanagh, "The Role of Ritual in Personal Development" in *The Roots of Ritual,* ed. Robert Bellah, et al. (Grand Rapids: Eerdmans, 1973), 145–60; Mark Searle, "Private Religion, Individualistic Society, and Common Worship," 27–46, and Robert W. Hovda, "Liturgy Forming Us in the Christian Life," 136–51, in *Liturgy and Spirituality in Context: Perspectives on Prayer and Culture,* ed. Eleanor Bernstein (Collegeville: Liturgical, 1990).

3. Charles P. Price and Louis Weil, *Liturgy for Living* (New York: Harper and Row, 1979), 21–23.

4. Geoffrey Wainwright, *Doxology* (New York: Oxford University Press, 1980), 8.

5. Alexander Schmemann, *Introduction to Liturgical Theology* (Crestwood, N.Y.: St. Vladimir's Seminary Press, 1986), 31.

6. James F. White, *Protestant Worship: Traditions in Transition* (Louisville: Westminster/John Knox, 1989), 209–16.

7. *Baptism, Ministry, and Eucharist* (Geneva: World Council of Churches, 1982), I, 1.

8. The ecumenical consensus on this matter is well articulated in *Baptism, Ministry, and Eucharist,* III, 32; a theological perspective is offered in *A Communion of Communions: One Eucharistic Fellowship,* ed. J. Robert Wright (New York: Seabury, 1979), e.g. xi–xii for basic assumptions; for a systematic theological perspective, see Wainwright, *Doxology,* e.g., 23–33.

9. At various times, almost always as a protest against abuses, the Eucharist has been abandoned or minimized as central to the community's worship. The constant reemergence of the Eucharist in community worship testifies to the intrinsic power of the sacrament to express the heart of Christian life. One may also suspect the involvement of the Holy Spirit.

10. Today, in light of the substantial numbers of nonchurched people in our society, some people have called for non-eucharistic worship as an ordinary form of worship for evangelic reasons. Because of increasing numbers of mixed marriages in which one partner is not Christian, others have proposed that the liturgy of the Word be the normative worship in order not to exclude such people from our corporate worship. To the first, I would respond that the Eucharist is not intended as an evangelistic service; the liturgy of the Word, however, may function to attract and inform those who are interested in the church but are not Christians. We also need to find better ways of reaching and evangelizing those who are unchurched or are nominally Christian. Taking the Eucharist from committed Christians does not, however, seem to me to be an appropriate way to proceed. I would make a similar response in the case of spouses and partners who are not Christian. However, I believe that we could profit from much more serious attention to appropriate hospitality for all committed believers of different faith traditions in the liturgy of the Word.

11. Gregory Dix, *The Shape of the Liturgy*, 1.

12. Aidan Kavanagh, *On Liturgical Theology* (New York: Pueblo, 1984), 4.

13. Alexander Schmemann, *Introduction to Liturgical Theology*, 31.

14. Bernard Iddings Bell, *The Altar and the World* (London: Dennis Dobson, 1948), 10–11.

15. *A Dictionary of Literary, Dramatic, and Cinematic Terms*, ed. Barnet, Berman, & Berto (Boston: Little, Brown, 1960, 1971), 38.

16. Northrop Frye, *Anatomy of Criticism* (Princeton: Princeton University Press, 1957), 268, 282–93.

17. Gordon W. Lathrop, *Holy Things: A Liturgical Theology* (Minneapolis: Fortress, 1993), 88–89.

18. Aristotle, "Poetics," *The Pocket Aristotle,* ed. Justin D. Kaplan (New York: Washington Square, 1958), 348. Aristotle wrote specifically of tragedy.

19. Karl F. Morrison, *The Mimetic Tradition of Reform in the West* (Princeton: Princeton University Press, 1982), 5–31.

20. Price and Weil, *Liturgy for Living*, 30–31, 34–37, 47–50; Avis, *Anglicanism and the Christian Church,* 8–10.

21. O. B. Hardison, *Christian Rite and Christian Drama in the Middle Ages* (Baltimore: Johns Hopkins University Press, 1965), 284–92.

22. *Book of Common Prayer,* 1979, 373.

23. For some of the different historical approaches, consult *The Study of the Liturgy,* ed. C. Jones, G. Wainwright, E. Yarnold (London: SPCK,1978), 147–288.

24. Geoffrey Wainwright, *Eucharist and Eschatology* (New York: Oxford University Press, 1981), 123–54.

25. Early church orders like the *Apostolic Constitutions* try to identify the different orders with persons of the Trinity, and the medievals tried to allegorize not only the orders, but each gesture with actions of God and Christ, as well as with different virtues, etc. O. B. Hardison, *Christian Rite and Christian Drama in the Middle Ages,* 34–90. On occasion this approach may have some merit, but usually it is quite misleading and distorting. The Eucharist is not a chronological reenacting of creation and redemption; it is a drama in which various elements are transformed and reshaped in context of the sacred sacrificial meal.

26. People from some Christian traditions will find these comments utterly irrelevant. But for Anglicans, Roman Catholics, and Orthodox, the allegorization of the roles of the Eucharist into human and divine is strong and alive. For instance, the priest is the icon of Jesus, which is why women purportedly cannot be ordained. The notion that the priest "plays" Jesus also reinforces clericalism, because the laity are only ordinary mortals in this rewriting of the script, while the clergy assume divine status during the Eucharist.

27. *Baptism, Eucharist, and Ministry,* I, 1.

28. Price and Weil, *Living for Liturgy,* 187.

29. Kenneth Stevenson, *Eucharist and Offering* (New York: Pueblo, 1986), 1–9.

30. Tissa Balasuriya, *The Eucharist and Human Liberation* (London: SCM Press, 1977); Anne Primavesi and Jennifer Henderson, *Our God Has No Favourites.*

31. Geoffrey Wainwright, *Eucharist and Eschatology,* 291–92.

32. Gregory Dix, *The Shape of the Liturgy,* 36–37; Oscar Cullmann, *Early Christian Worship* (Naperville, Ill.: Allenson, 1953), 26–32; Reginald Fuller, *What Is Liturgical Preaching?* (London: SCM Press, 1957), 18–22, recapitulates the argument. James White, *A Brief History of Christian Worship* (Nashville: Abingdon, 1993), 24–30, suggests that the Eucharist, arising from a Jewish ritual meal, would have

prayers, blessings, and some Scripture in its earliest form, even if not the synaxis and the eucharistic liturgy of the later first and second century.

33. Theodor Klauser, *A Short History of the Western Liturgy* (Oxford: Oxford University Press, 1979), 149.

34. Gerard S. Sloyan, *Worshipful Preaching* (Philadelphia: Fortress, 1984); William Skudlarek (Nashville: Abingdon, 1981). Peter C. Bower's *Handbook for the Common Lectionary* (Philadelphia: Geneva Press, 1987) represents an effort to restore more integrity to the connection of preaching and liturgy even in those churches who do not celebrate the Eucharist each Sunday.

35. Patricia Wilson-Kastner, *Imagery for Preaching* (Minneapolis: Fortress, 1989), 11–31, provides a summary of the development and some of the major influences.

36. Eugene L. Lowry, *The Homiletical Plot* (Atlanta: John Knox, 1980), 25.

2. People, Time, and Space: The Inclusive Community

1. *The Catechumenal Process.* (New York: Church Hymnal Corporation, 1990), 1–15.

2. Patricia Wilson-Kastner, "Preaching and Inclusiveness," *Breaking the Word,* ed. Carl Daw (New York: Church Hymnal Society, 1994).

3. *For the Sake of the Kingdom: God's Church and the New Creation,* Inter-Anglican Theological and Doctrinal Commission (London: Anglican Consultative Council, 1986), 4–14.

4. E.g., Mark R. Francis, *Liturgy in a Multicultural Community* (Collegeville, Minn.: Liturgical, 1991); *How Shall We Pray?* ed. Ruth A. Meyers (New York: Church Hymnal Corp., 1994).

5. The disciplinary rubrics in the American *Book of Common Prayer* offer a useful direction. The only exclusions from Communion are a notoriously evil life, a phrase that has certain dangers, but if taken seriously includes only the most vicious of unrepentant people; those people who have done wrong to their neighbor but will not make restitution, and those who are embroiled in conflict and refuse to forgive the other and repair the damage. The standards are charity, desire to do good, and loyalty to the community; exclusion from the life of the community is only allowed when the person in question seems to be destroying the life of the particular community in identifiable ways.

6. Mircea Eliade, *The Sacred and the Profane: The Nature of Religion* (New York: Harper and Row, 1959), 11–15, 162–213; idem, *Patterns in Comparative Religion* (Cleveland: World Pub./Meridian, 1958, 1963), 1–37.

7. Mircea Eliade, *Myth and Reality* (New York: Harper and Row, 1963), esp. 75–91; *Cosmos and History* (New York: Harper and Row, 1959), 139–62.

8. Augustine of Hippo, *Confessions,* trans. Rex Warner (New York: New American Library/Mentor Omega, 1963), XX-XIII, 210–350.

9. Thomas Aquinas, *Summa Theologiae* (Turin: Marietti, 1952), I, 2, a.3; 7, a.1–4. Thomas asserted that God could be eternal and the creator even if the world were temporally infinite, because God's creative activity was causal, not dependent on having to exist before the time of creation. However, Thomas believed that the world had been created in time, with a beginning and end, because of the testimony of revelation, not because of the intrinsic structure of the universe.

10. Augustine, *Confessions*, 217–35.

11. Anthony Aveni, *Empires of Time* (New York: Basic, 1989), 5–6. Stephen W. Hawking, *A Brief History of Time* (New York: Bantam, 1988); and Richard Morris, *Time's Arrows* (New York: Simon and Schuster, 1984), provide historical perspective and an introduction to modern theories about time.

12. Ibid., 85–90.

13. Ibid., 338–39.

14. David Ulansey, *The Origins of the Mithraic Mysteries* (New York: Oxford, 1989), esp. 93–94, offers such a perspective on the rise and popularity of Mithraism.

15. See, for instance, G. B. Caird, *The Language and Imagery of the Bible* (Philadelphia: Westminster, 1980), 201–71.

16. Thomas J. Talley, *The Origins of the Liturgical Year* (New York: Pueblo, 1986), 231–32.

17. Peter G. Cobb, "The Calendar," in *The Study of Liturgy*, ed. C. Jones, G. Wainwright, E. Yarnold (London: SPCK, 1978), 404.

18. W. K. Lowther Clarke, "The Calendar," *Liturgy and Worship,* ed. W. K. Lowther Clarke (London: SPCK, 1932, 1981), 201-39; Cobb, "The Christian Year," *The Study of Liturgy,* 403–19.

19. Gregory Dix, *The Shape of the Liturgy* (London: Dacre, 1945, 1975), 350–53.

20. Pierre Teilhard de Chardin, *The Future of Man* (New York: Harper and Row, 1959, 1964), esp. 312–23.

21. James White, *Protestant Worship: Traditions in Transition* (Louisville: Westminster/John Knox, 1989), 67.

22. Ibid., 77–78, 132–34.

23. D. J. Bartholomew, *God of Chance* (London: SCM, 1984); Paul Davies, *The Cosmic Blueprint* (New York: Simon and Schuster, 1988); James Gleick, *Chaos* (New York: Viking, 1987); Nick Herbert, *Quantum Reality* (Garden City, N.Y.: Anchor Press/Doubleday, 1985), offer popular versions of the scientific quest for the order, or purposelessness, behind the universe.

24. Alan Dunstan, *Interpreting Worship* (Wilton, Conn.: Morehouse Barlow, 1985), 2.

25. Aidan Kavanagh, *On Liturgical Theology* (New York: Pueblo, 1984), 8.

26. Louis Duch, "The Experience and Symbolism of Time," in *The Times of Celebration*, ed. David Power (New York: Seabury, 1981), 26–28.

27. Bernard Iddings Bell, *The Altar and the World* (London: Dennis Dobson, 1946), 9.

28. A. G. Herbert, *Liturgy and Society* (London: Faber and Faber, 1935), 70.

29. Kavanagh, *On Liturgical Theology*, 173.

30. Thomas Stearnes Eliot, *Collected Poems: 1909–1962* (London: Faber, 1963), 215.

31. Eliade, *The Sacred and the Profane*, 22–27.

32. Graydon F. Snyder, *Ante Pacem* (Macon, Ga.: Mercer University Press), 67–117.

33. Cobb, "The Architectural Setting of the Liturgy," in *The Study of the Liturgy*, ed. Jones, Wainwright, Yarnold, 474; Marion J. Hatchett, *Sanctifying Life, Time and Space: An Introduction to Liturgical Study* (New York: Seabury, 1976), 28–29, 49–50.

34. Alexander Schmemann, *Introduction to Liturgical Theology* (Crestwood, N.Y.: St. Vladimir's Seminary Press, 1986), 114.

35. Ibid., 114-18; Cobb, "The Architectural Setting,"475–76.

36. Schmemann, *Introduction to Liturgical Theology*, 114–18; Cobb, "The Architectural Setting," 475–77.

37. Cobb, "The Architectural Setting," 477–80; Hatchett, *Sanctifying*

Life, Time and Space, 177–79; James White, *Introduction to Christian Worship* (rev. ed.; Nashville: Abingdon, 1990), 76–97.

38. Peter Hammond, *Liturgy and Architecture* (London: Barrie and Rockliff, 1960), 1–11, 154–73; F. Debeyst, "Architectural Setting (Modern) and the Liturgical Movement," in *The New Westminster Dictionary of Liturgy and Worship* (Philadelphia: Westminster, 1986), 36–48.

39. White, *Introduction to Christian Worship,* 76.

40. Nicolas Zernov, *Eastern Christendom* (London: Weidenfeld and Nicolson, 1961), 260–61.

3. The Word and the World: God's People at Worship and Work

1. Wade Clark Roof and William McKinney, *American Mainline Religion* (New Brunswick, N.J.: Rutgers University Press, 1988), 170–71.

2. J. Russell Hale, *The Unchurched: Who They Are and Why They Stay Away* (San Francisco: Harper and Row, 1980); Edward A. Rauff, *Why People Join the Church* (New York: Pilgrim, 1970), 50–60.

3. Roof and McKinney, *American Mainline Religion,* 244–49.

4. J. G. Davies, "Baptistery," in *A Dictionary of Liturgy and Worship,* ed. J. G. Davies (London: SCM, 1972), 68–73.

5. This notion of our cosmic role to pray on behalf of all creation is found in such biblical texts in the liturgy as the Song of the Children in the Fiery Furnace (inserted in the Book of Daniel), and in the Exultet of the Easter Vigil. The 1976 American *Book of Common Prayer* provides one example in Prayer C of Eucharistic Rite II, and *Book of Worship United Church of Christ* offers another in Communion Prayer A of "Service of Word and Sacrament II." Teilhard de Chardin's "Mass on the World" (Pierre Teilhard de Chardin, *The Heart of Matter* [New York: Harcourt Brace Jovanovich, 1978], 119–34) vividly expresses the same sentiments of humanity's praying on behalf of the whole creation.

6. Mircea Eliade, The *Sacred and the Profane: The Nature of Religion* (New York: Harper and Row, 1959), 25–27; idem, *Shamanism* (Princeton, N.J.: Princeton University Press, 1964), 482–94. Urban Holmes, *Ministry and Imagination* (New York: Seabury, 1981), 87–191, adapted some of Eliade's notion of liminality in his theology of priesthood. However, as Holmes noted, for the Christian the shamanic dimension of priesthood is representative for all Christians, not exclusively constitutive of the ordained.

7. In that sense, worship is not liminal but rather celebrates a reality that is already present. However, because human beings are beings of time and space and sequence, as well as at every moment interwoven with God and the ordinary, we need times and places of special focus. We need to "enter into" worship distinguished but not separated from everyday life.

8. Paul Avis, *Anglicanism and the Christian Church* (Minneapolis: Fortress, 1989), 1-20.

9. Dante, *The Divine Comedy 3: Paradise,* trans. Dorothy Sayers and Barbara Reynolds (New York: Penguin, 1962), 303-49, cantos 28-33.

10. John A. T. Robinson, *Liturgy Coming to Life* (London: Mowbray, 1960), 29.

11. Ibid.

12. Perhaps this is as good a place as any to address the accusation made in various forms of liberation theology that liturgy can be a form of oppression, rather than transformation. For instance, Margerie Procter-Smith*, In Her Own Rite* (Nashville: Abingdon, 1990), 136-63, as a feminist theologian, and Tissa Balasuriya, *The Eucharist and Human Liberation* (London: SCM, 1977), 1-9, from the perspective of a liberation theologian. My intent here is not to explore the history of the abuses and oppression that liturgies in fact did sanctify, or to examine all the different oppressive systems that the institutional church supported. Liturgies (and the churches that celebrate them) have been and are agents of oppression. My goal in this book is to accept the centrality of the eucharistic liturgy, grounded in and arising from the living tradition of a scripturally authentic church (or as much of one as we can have in this life). I assume as axiomatic that God is revealed to us through the Scriptures, and that the Scriptures offer the primary authentication of our liturgies. Liturgy, like the church, ought to be *semper reformanda,* and a thorough scriptural scrutiny, in the light of our church's experience and reflection over the centuries and our own encounter with our society should provide ample reformation for any oppressive system or individual action.

13. Gregory Dix, *The Shape of the Liturgy* (London: Dacre, 1945, 1975)*,* 38–47.

14. C. P. M. Jones, "The Eucharist: The New Testament," in *The Study of Liturgy,* ed. C. Jones, G. Wainwright, and E. Yarnold (London: SPCK, 1978), 154–55.

15. Dix, *The Shape of the Liturgy,* 38.

16. "Didache," in *Apostolic Fathers,* trans. Kirsop Lake (Cambridge, Mass.: Harvard University Press, 1912, 1970), 1:9, 322.

17. Craig Douglas Erickson, *Participating in Worship* (Louisville: Westminster/John Knox, 1989), 65.

18. Every contemporary denominational worship book recommends an explicit confession of sins as a part of the eucharistic liturgy, with the exception of Epiphanytide and Easter to Pentecost. The difference of opinion is about the placement of the confession, whether just after the Opening Greeting (as do the Roman Catholics and most Protestants) or after the Prayers of the People and before the Peace, as a preparation for Communion (Anglican tradition).

19. Richard Swinburne, *Revelation* (Oxford: Clarendon, 1992), is one of the most recent volumes to raise questions about what revelation is, competing religious truths, and criteria for determining which biblical passages ought to be interpreted literally and which metaphorically. Libraries are filled with efforts to understand, refute, and defend various interpretations of revelation. My primary concern is with very basic issues about the possibility of revelation.

20. "By Whose Authority?" by Ellen Wondra, a paper delivered at the September 1991 meeting of the Conference of Anglican Theologians, excellently analyzed the situation from the perspective of a feminist critique. For the perspective of liberation theologies, one might consult Elsa Tamez, *Bible of the Oppressed* (Maryknoll: Orbis, 1982), or Itumelung J. Mosala, *Biblical Hermeneutics and Black Theology in South Africa* (Grand Rapids: Eerdmans, 1989).

21. Phyllis Trible, *God and the Rhetoric of Sexuality* (Philadelphia: Fortress, 1978), 1–30.

22. Reginald Fuller, "Lectionary," in *A Dictionary of Liturgy and Worship,* 211-12, offers a good brief overview of the development of lectionaries.

23. Lectionaries can and do also cut out from consideration important parts of the biblical story. For instance, much of the story of women in the Bible is not in the assigned lectionary readings for Sundays. That omission already demonstrates the limitations and/or sexist bias of the compilers of the lectionary readings. As perusal of the history of lectionaries will show, they are not fixed in stone, although a few traditions, such as the use of John during Holy Week, seem fairly well fixed.

24. A. G. Hebert, *Liturgy and Society* (London: Faber and Faber, 1935), 67.

25. Lay-led Bible studies, informed by reliable biblical scholarship, are a promising development. For instance, Liturgical Press distributes the Little Rock series, which uses the Liturgical Press Commentaries. Bethel Bible Series is less sophisticated but very usable in congregations.

26. Henry Mitchell, *The Recovery of Preaching* (New York: Harper and Row, 1977), 37.

27. Elizabeth Canham, *Praying the Bible* (Boston: Cowley, 1987), is one useful introduction to biblically based prayer, especially helpful for those who feel anxious or uncertain about how to pray with the Scriptures.

28. I have no intention of entering the complex debate about private and corporate prayer. In real life, we pray or we do not pray. If we are fully human, we pray privately (whether that be in an organized or haphazard fashion) and we pray corporately, because we are both social and individual.

29. Erickson, *Participating in Worship,* 40-52, offers an assessment of the value of silence. His analysis holds value for every tradition and style of worship.

30. E.g., *The Wideness of God's Mercy,* ed. Jeffery W. Rowthorn, 2 vols. (New York: Seabury, 1985).

31. Alan Richardson, "Creed, Creeds," *A Dictionary of Liturgy and Worship,* 156.

32. Geoffrey Wainwright, *Doxology* (New York: Oxford, 1980), 182–98.

33. For a fourth-century example, consider the story of Synesius of Cyrene, recounted in Hans von Campenhausen, *The Fathers of the Greek Church* (New York: Pantheon, 1955, 1959), 122–26.

34. Gilbert Cope, "The Kiss of Peace and the Pax" in "Gestures," *A Dictionary of Liturgy and Worship,* 187-89; Erickson, *Participating in Worship,* 29-31; Dix, *The Shape of the Liturgy,* 105–10.

4. Preaching: Incarnational Prayer

1. *Sermon* has its roots in the Latin word for *word,* and *homily* in the Greek word for conversation. Substantively, each word means the same thing. However, in modern American usage, the term *homily* is

usually employed for a brief address on the Scripture (usually the Gospel) at the Eucharist; *sermon* is the term for a more substantive address to the congregation about the Scriptures in the context of worship, eucharistic or non-eucharistic. I am using the term *sermon* in part because it is the most common outside the Roman Catholic Church, and also because I believe it at present to be a more encompassing term.

2. Reginald Fuller, *What Is Liturgical Preaching?* (London: SCM, 1957); Geoffrey Wainwright, "Preaching as Worship" in *Theories of Preaching: Selected Readings in the Homiletical Tradition*, ed. Richard Lischer (Durham: Labyrinth, 1987), 353–63; Patricia Wilson-Kastner, *Imagery for Preaching* (Minneapolis: Fortress, 1989), 95–102.

3. J. Hei, "Preaching in the Talmudic Period," in *Encyclopedia Judaica,* ed. Cecil Roth and Geoffrey Wigoder (Philadelphia: Coronet, 1994), vol. 13, col. 994.

4. Jacob Neusner, *A Rabbi Talks with Jesus: An Intermillennial, Interfaith Exchange* (New York: Doubleday, 1994).

5. "The First Apology of Justin Martyr," 67, in *Liturgies of the Western Church,* ed. Bard Thompson (Philadelphia: Fortress, 1981), 9.

6. Henry Mitchell, *The Recovery of Preaching* (San Francisco: Harper, 1977), 74–95.

7. William Skudlarek, *The Word in Worship* (Nashville: Abingdon, 1981), 92-96; David J. Schlaffer, *Surviving the Sermon* (Boston: Cowley, 1992), 3–14.

8. Mitchell, *The Recovery of Preaching,* 115–23.

9. "Epistle to Diognetus," in *Apostolic Fathers*, ed. Kirsop Lake (Cambridge, Mass.: Harvard University Press, 1970), II, sec. 6–7, offers an early articulation of this Christian experience.

10. Patricia Wilson-Kastner, "Pastoral Theology and the Lord's Prayer" in *The Lord's Prayer,* ed. Daniel L. Migliore (Grand Rapids: Eerdmans, 1993), 107–24.

11. E.g., Schlaffer, *Surviving the Sermon.*

12. Stephen L. Carter, *The Culture of Disbelief: How American Law and Politics Trivialize Religious Devotion* (New York: Basic, 1993). Carter's study is more negative about the place of religion in American contemporary culture than I think is justified. However, his central point about the social acceptability of the demeaning of religion and devotion is well taken. Any preacher who wishes to preach effectively

will be aware of this popular atmosphere and help believers to address it in everyday life.

13. Gregory Dix, *The Shape of the Liturgy* (London: Dacre, 1945, 1975), 36–102, argues for an original disconnection between liturgy of the Word and of the Sacrament. Oscar Cullman, *Early Christian Worship* (Napierville, Ill.: Alec R. Allenson, 1953, 1956), 26–32, argues the contrary, and his view is accepted by most scholars today.

14. Thomas H. Keir, *The Word in Worship* (London: Oxford University Press, 1962), 35.

15. Wilson-Kastner, *Imagery for Preaching,* 100–101.

16. Gerald S. Sloyan, *Worshipful Preaching* (Philadelphia: Fortress, 1984), 11–17.

17. This cursory description is derived from such theorists as Carter, *The Culture of Disbelief,* esp. 23–101, 263–74; Gordon S. Wood, *The Radicalism of the American Revolution* (New York: Knopf, 1992), 229–369; Robert Bellah et al., *The Good Society* (New York: Vintage/Random House, 1992), 179–286.

18. Inter-Anglican Theological and Doctrinal Commission, *For the Sake of the Kingdom: God's Church and the New Creation* (Cincinnati: Forward Movement, 1986).

19. Thomas Stearns Eliot, "Choruses from the Rock," in *Collected Poems 1909–1963* (London: Faber and Faber, 1963), 170.

20. James L. Empereur and Christopher G. Keisling, *The Liturgy That Does Justice* (Collegeville, Minn.: Michael Glazier, 1990), 85–89.

21. Ibid., 93.

22. *The Church Is All of You,* ed. J. R. Brockman (London: Collins, 1984), 73.

5. Eucharist: Communion and Community

1. Charles Williams, "At the 'Ye that do truly,'" *The New Oxford Book of Christian Verse,* ed. Donald Davie (Oxford: Oxford University Press, 1981), 257.

2. Alice Meynall, "The Unknown God," *The Poems of Alice Meynall* (New York: Charles Scribners Sons, 1924), 78.

3. Paul Tillich, *The Courage to Be* (New Haven: Yale University Press, 1952), esp. 32–63, 155–90, identified briefly these basic metaphors for a relationship to God; liturgically, they are expressed most intensely in the Eucharist.

4. *Baptism, Eucharist, and Ministry* (Geneva: World Council of Churches, 1982) identifies a group of ideas rather than images: The Eucharist as Thanksgiving to the Father, an Anemnesis or Memorial of Christ, Invocation of the Spirit, Communion of the Faithful, Meal of the Kingdom (sec. II, no. 2–26). One can integrate the *BEM* theological interpretation with the image of the sacrificial meal, although most liturgies focus on one or more interpretations, with the other elements expressed less prominently.

5. Michael Downey, *Clothed in Christ* (New York: Crossroad, 1987), 86–90.

6. Kenneth Stevenson, *Eucharist and Offering* (New York: Pueblo, 1986), 235; see also Ernest Falardeau, *A Holy and Living Sacrifice: The Eucharist in Christian Perspective* (Collegeville, Minn.: Liturgical, 1996), 3–8.

7. W. Jardine Grisbroke, "Anaphora," in *The New Westminster Dictionary of Liturgy and Worship* (Philadelphia: Westminster, 1986), 18.

8. Gordon Lathrop, *Holy Things: A Liturgical Theology* (Minneapolis: Fortress, 1993), 139–58.

9. John Deane, "The Offertory," in *The Deer's Cry*, ed. Patrick Murray (Dublin: Four Courts, 1986), 263–64.

10. Stevenson, *Eucharist and Offering*, 13.

11. Jacob Neusner, *A Rabbi Talks with Jesus: An Intermillennial, Interfaith Exchange* (New York: Doubleday, 1993), 116–32.

12. James F. White, *A History of Christian Worship* (Nashville: Abingdon, 1993), 24–26.

13. Charles Avila, *Ownership: Early Christian Teaching* (Maryknoll: Orbis, 1983), 151.

14. Stevenson, *Eucharist and Offering*, 36–37, 236.

15. O. B. Hardison, *Christian Rite and Christian Drama in the Middle Ages*, 35–40; Eamon Duffy, *The Stripping of the Altars* (New Haven: Yale University Press, 1992), 233–98.

16. Edward Foley, *From Age to Age* (Chicago: Liturgy Training Programs, 1991), 114–37.

17. Geoffrey Wainwright, "Recent Eucharistic Revision," in *The Study of the Liturgy*, ed. C. Jones, G. Wainwright, and E. Yarnold (London: SPCK, 1978), 280–88.

18. Robert Bocock, *Ritual in Industrial Society* (London: George Allen and Unwin, 1974), 75.

19. Arthur Michael Ramsey, *God, Christ and the World* (London: SCM, 1969), esp. 105–117, analyzes this trend and Christian response; Elizabeth Johnson, *She Who Is* (New York: Crossroad, 1993), 191–273, addresses the question from a feminist theological perspective, which questions classical definitions of divine transcendence and immanence.

20. Bocock, *Ritual in Industrial Society*, 80.

21. Ibid., 83–84.

22. Gregory Dix, *The Shape of the Liturgy* (London: Dacre, 1945, 1975), 48.

23. J. G. Davies, *Everyday God: Encountering the Holy in World and Worship* (London: SCM, 1973), 340–41.

24. John A. T. Robinson, *On Being the Church in the World* (London: SCM, 1960), 60.

25. Dix, *The Shape of the Liturgy*, 111–23.

26. Stevenson, *Eucharist and Offering*, 224–25. Charles Wheatly, *A Rational Illustration of the* Book of Common Prayer *of the Church of England* (Oxford: Thomas Tegg, 1839), 268–74, argues for the integrity of the offertory of bread and wine and alms, as well as insisting on the direct connection between the ritual action and the ethical economic consequences.

27. Bernard Iddings Bell, *The Altar and the World* (London: Dennis Dobson, 1948), 31–32.

28. *Baptism, Eucharist, and Ministry*, "Eucharist," III, 27, notes these elements as being "in varying sequence and of diverse importance."

29 A. G. Hebert, *Liturgy and Society* (London: Faber and Faber, 1935), 195.

30. Geoffrey Wainwright, *Eucharist and Eschatology* (New York: Oxford University Press, 1981), esp. 147–54.

31. Ibid., 151–53.

32. Anne Primavesi and Jennifer Henderson, *Our God Has No Favourites* (Tunbridge Wells, Eng.: Burns & Oates, 1989), 68.

33. J. A. T. Robinson, *Liturgy Coming to Life* (London: Mowbray, 1960), 31.

34. Lucien Deiss, *Early Sources of the Liturgy* (Collegeville, Minn.: Liturgical, 1967), 63.

35. Iddings Bell, *The Altar and the World.*

6. The World Becoming Itself: Liturgy and the Future

1. Isak Dinesen, *Anecdotes of Destiny and Ehrengard* (New York: Vintage International/Random House, 1993), 21–59.

2. Norman Cohn, *Cosmos, Chaos, and the World to Come* (New Haven: Yale University Press, 1993), 3–4, 105–15, 220–26.

3. Richard H. Hiers, "Eschatology," in *Harper's Bible Dictionary,* ed. Paul Achtemeier (San Francisco: Harper and Row, 1985), 275–77.

4. Karl Rahner, "Eschatology," *Encyclopedia of Theology: The Concise Sacramentum Mundi* (New York: Seabury, 1975), 434–39.

5. C. H. Dodd, *The Parables of the Kingdom* (London: Religious Book Club, 1942), 51.

6. Bernard McGinn, *Anti-Christ* (San Francisco: Harper, 1994), 12–13; John Dominic Crossan, *Who Killed Jesus?* (San Francisco: Harper, 1995), 46–47.

7. Colleen McDannell and Bernhard Lang, *Heaven: A History* (New Haven: Yale University Press, 1988), 276–358.

8. Don E. Saliers, *Worship as Theology: Foretaste of Divine Glory* (Nashville: Abingdon, 1994), 51.

9. *For the Sake of the Kingdom: God's Church and the New Creation,* Inter-Anglican Theological and Doctrinal Commission (London: Anglican Consultative Council, 1986), 13–18.

10. Shen Mah (Archbishop Torkom Manoogian), *The Arc* (New York: St. Vartan's, 1983), n.p.

11. Rowan Williams, "Imagining the Kingdom" in *The Identity of Anglican Worship,* ed. Kenneth Stephenson and Bryan Spinks (Harrisburg, Pa.: Morehouse, 1991), 3.

12. Helen Oppenheimer, *The Hope of Heaven* (Cambridge, Mass.: Cowley, 1988), 148.

13. Saliers, *Worship as Theology,* 61.

14. Ibid.

15. Gordon Lathrop, *Holy Things: A Liturgical Theology* (Minneapolis: Fortress, 1993), 207.

16. Ibid., 217.

17. Saliers, *Worship as Theology,* 173.

18. Geervarghese Mar Osthathios, *Theology of a Classless Society* (Guildford and London: Lutterworth, 1979), 66.

19. McDannell and Lang, *Heaven: A History,* 358.

20. *Book of Worship United Church of Christ,* 1986, 48.

21. Samuel Ryan outlines a comprehensive theological perspective in "The Earth Is the Lord's," *Ecotheology: Voices from North and South,* ed. David G. Hallman (Geneva: WCC Publications, 1994), 130–48.

22. Pierre Teilhard de Chardin, *The Future of Man* (New York: Harper and Row, 1964), 85–144.

23. Geoffrey Wainwright, *Eucharist and Eschatology* (New York: Oxford University Press, 1981), 147–51.

24. Mark R. Francis, *Liturgy in a Multicultural Community* (Collegeville, Minn.: Liturgical, 1991), 9–19; Juan Oliver, "Language Shaped and Shaping," in *How Shall We Pray?* ed. Ruth Meyers (New York: Church Hymnal Society, 1994), 136–53.

25. Pierre Teilhard de Chardin, "The Mass on the World," in *Hymn of the Universe* (New York: Harper and Row, 1961), 19–37. Grace Jantzen, *God's World, God's Body* (Philadelphia: Westminster, 1984), rejects philosophical and theological dualism and proposes considering creation as God's body, in analogy with the body and spirit of humanity. Jantzen's focus is theocentric; Teilhard's is explicitly eucharistic and trinitarian. Vladimir Soloviev, *Lectures on Godmanhood* (London: Dobson, 1948), explores a vision of Sophia that parallels in some significant ways Teilhard's Christology; for Soloviev, Sophia is at the same time the "world soul, the ideal humanity, the principle of created nature; and on the other hand, 'Sophia is the body of God, the matter of divinity, permeated with the beginning of divine unity'" (p. 59).

26. Teilhard, "The Mass on the World," in *Hymn of the Universe,* 19.

27. Ibid., 22–23.

28. Ibid., 35–36.

Epilogue

1. Gordon S. Wood, *The Radicalism of the American Revolution* (New York: Alfred Knopf, 1992), 347–69.

2. Robert N. Bellah, Richard Madsen, et al., *The Good Society* (New York: Random House/Vintage, 1992), 254–86.

3. Paul H. Jones, "We Are How We Worship: Corporate Worship as a Matrix for Christian Identity Formation," in *Worship* 69: 4 (July 1995), 346–60.

Index